Natural Learning From A to Z

Thematic Activities and Phonemic Awareness Emphasis for Letters and Letter Sounds

By Mary Jo Ayres

Natural Learning Publications
Leland, Mississippi

Cover illustration and graphics by Creative Visions
Cleveland, MS
Illustrated by Lauren Brain

Library of Congress Catalog Card Number 09-75610
ISBN 0-9661298-0-6

PRINTED IN THE UNITED STATES OF AMERICA

It is an honor for me to share my ideas with you. I hope that this book will be very useful to you and a lot of fun as you encourage *Natural Learning* for the children in your class. I would like to thank Dr. Janie Allen-Bradley for her help with my book and, I would like to thank the many teachers, friends, and family members who have encouraged me. I would like to express deep love and appreciation to my husband, Stanley, and my children, Elizabeth and Will, who have supported me, laughed with me, and put up with me! I love y'all!

Happy Teaching,

Mary Jo Ayres

Natural Learning
Mary Jo Ayres
103 Sycamore St.
Leland, MS 38756

If you would like information about a *Natural Learning* workshop or keynote:
Phone: 601-686-9691
e-mail: nlearn@tecinfo.com   **Web site:** http://www.tecinfo.com/~nlearn
Fax: 601-686-2365

Table of Contents:

Letter A Investigations:

- **Learn about animals, antelope, alligators, and anteaters.**
- **Learn about ants. (Have an ant farm in your room.)**
- **Learn about apples.**
- **Learn about Johnny Appleseed.**
- **Learn about astronauts.**

Art:

⇒ Mold an "Alice" or "Albert" the Alligator with green dough or paint dough green.

⇒ Draw or paint ants on a page. (Compare who drew many or few.)

⇒ Apple Stamps: Cut apples different ways and dip apples in paint.

⇒ Draw a picture and let children use animal crackers to move around the picture. Let children tell about their animals and story.

⇒ Make astronaut helmets. (See art p.149)

Tactile:

* Let children trace an uppercase "A" with a marker. Let children draw an ant at the top to indicate where to begin writing an "A." May use a raisin and draw legs to make ant at top. Let children run their finger down the "A" to show how the ant would run to make the lines in an "A."

Baking:

◊ Make ant cookies (raisin cookies). Pretend they are ants.

◊ Make apple tarts or baked apples.

Counting:

♥ Discover few or many with the ant pictures.

♥ Does an apple have few or many apple seeds? (Use the apples you used to paint with.)

♥ Does an alligator have few or many teeth?

♥ Count pretend ants (raisins).

Games:

- "Aunt Alice Says" (alias "Simon Says")
- Apple Hunt: Cut out construction paper apples and hide in room. Let children look for the apples. Then count how many they find.
- Apple Pie: Take a tin pie pan and put some construction paper apples in bottom of tin. Let children pass it around while a song is played. When the music stops, the child with the plate says a word that begins with short sound of "A."

Fieldtrips and Special Days:

- ➢ Visit an airport.
- ➢ Take a walk and look for some ants on the sidewalk.
- ➢ Go on an Adventure Walk.
- ➢ Pretend to be astronauts going to outer space.

Books:

I Can't Said the Ant by Polly Cameron
Alligator's Toothache by Diane De Groat
A Is For Anything: An ABC Book of Pictures & Rhymes by Katharina Barry
An Animal for Alan by Edward R. Ricciuti

Songs:

| Tune to: | **"Oh, Do you Know the Muffin Man?"** |
| Song: | **"Alphabet Song"** |

Oh, do you know the alphabet, the alphabet, the alphabet? Oh, do you know the alphabet, that starts with Letter "A?" (/a/ sound optional at end of song.)

Andy picked an apple, an apple, an apple. Andy picked an apple and made an apple pie.
(Second verse, use girl's name Alice) First time reach up and pick apples with right hand and second time reach with left hand. Then hold hands together as a pie. How many apples did you pick when singing the song once? (twice)

Tune to: "Twinkle, Twinkle Little Star"
Song: "Adventure Song"

After I eat my apple pie, an adventure I might try.
Off to Africa I might go, imagination is never slow.
Anteaters, antelopes, animals I see.
What an adventure is waiting for me!

Tune to: "Jimmy Crack Corn"
Song: "Astronaut Song"

I'm an astronaut flying in space
Going in my rocket ship to some place.
Maybe landing on Pluto,
I'm just ready to go!
(Wave arms as if flying)

Fingerplay:

One little acrobat swinging through the air.
(Hold index finger up and swing side to side.)

He flips and he flops as we stare.
(Make index finger bend up and down.)

And suddenly he's caught by another with flare!
(Excitement in voice, lock both index fingers together.)

He didn't even know that he gave me a scare!
(Shake head and wipe brow.)

One little acrobat swinging through the air.
(Hold index finger up and swing side to side.)

He lands and bows with the greatest of care!
(With left palm facing up, place right hand with index finger up on left palm and bend it as to bow.)

Anxious Ants

10 little ants wanting food to eat	(Wiggle 10 fingers.)
Found a summer picnic, what a treat!	(Clap on treat.)
5 took a sweet	(5 fingers pretend to get sweet.)
and 5 began to eat.	(Bring other hand to mouth.)
and the 10 little ants went down the street!	(Wiggle all ten fingers.)

Adventurous Astronauts

Ten astronauts in a rocket ship
(Hold up 10 fingers and then let fingertips touch to point like rocket.)

Flying through space gonna make a little trip.
(Keep point of rocket with fingers and weave back and forth.)

Going past Mars and Jupiter, too.
(Keep hands the same.)

Ten little astronauts, what a crew!
(Hold up 10 fingers.)

Apples

Little red apples falling from the tree.	(Wiggle fingers downward.)
Before I knew it I ate three.	(Hold up three finger on one hand.)
Then I ate another two	(Hold up two fingers on other hand.)
And I was feeling kinda blue.	(Rub tummy.)
How many apples did I eat?	
1 2 3 4 5	(Touch five fingertips.)

Always acknowledge children whose first or last name begins with letter that you are emphasizing.

NOTES:

Letter B Investigations:

- **Learn about butterflies.**
- **Learn about bees and bumblebees.**
- **Learn about birds.**
- **Learn about buffaloes.**
- **Learn about beavers.**
- **Learn about bears.**

Art:

⇒ Make a bear book, perhaps with blue or brown construction paper. Cut out bears using different material such as sandpaper or a smooth material. On one page, glue only on three edges of a square piece of material as to be a quilt on a bed. Let children put the different bears that they have cut out in the bed. Use "Bears in Bed" fingerplay and "Bears in the Bed" song.
(Cut out Baby Bear on p.159)

⇒ Make bear pictures with different textures and colors. Make bow tie of one material or color. Cut soft material for inside of ears. Glue buttons for eyes or let children paint or color eyes blue, brown, or black.

⇒ Make bulletin boards using the cardboard that fabric is draped around in stores. (Contact a material store to save them for you.) Glue bows or baseball cards on top of bulletin boards.

Tactile:

∗ Draw letter "Bb" on cardboard, let children apply glue and put beans on glue for a beanie "B."

Baking:

◊ Bake blueberry muffins.
◊ Make banana bread.
◊ Make bean soup.
◊ Bake canned biscuits. On the uncooked biscuits, let children paint a bear face with food coloring.
◊ Let children put butter on their biscuit.

Counting:

♥ Count or sort buttons or beans.

♥ Make bead bracelets with pipe cleaner and slide-on beads. Emphasize patterns of two or three. (Example: blue, red, blue, red, etc.)

♥ Cut out bread pattern and let children glue or paint 5 blueberries.

Games:

• Burst the balloon with your bottom. (relay game) Blow up balloons and divide children into groups. Put chairs at a certain distance from rows of children. Have helpers at the chairs to hand balloon to runner. Runner must burst the balloon by sitting on it and return to line.

• Make bean bags with zip lock bags. (Glue top or fold top over and staple.) Throw beanbags in a bucket.

• Play Bear Bingo. Cut out bear pattern in different colors. Draw different amounts of dots on bears' bellies. Give three bears to each child. Duplicate bears and dots and put in another bag to draw from. Draw Bear and say "Red bear (3)", "Green bear (5)," etc. If children have the bear called out, they can move the bear to the side. When all three bears are moved to the side, the child can call out "Bear Bingo."

Fieldtrips and Special Days:

➢ Visit a bank or a bakery.

➢ Pretend to go on a bear hunt.

➢ Contact your state forestry agency or your local National Forest Office for the "Smokey Bear" program for your school. Remember that Smokey's main objective is educating the public in preventing humanly caused forest fires.

➢ Let children bring their baby picture for "Beautiful Baby Bulletin Board." Be sure child's name is on back. Let children try to guess who each baby is.

Books:

Bedtime for Bears by Adelaide Hall Garrard
Benjy's Blanket by Myra Berry Brown
Ten Bears in my Bed by Stanley Mack
Big Bad Bruce by Bill Peet
How Big is a Brachiosaurus? by Susan Carroll
How Many Bugs in a Box? by David A. Carter

Songs:

Tune to: **"London Bridge"**
Song: **"Bouncing "B"**

Baby has a bouncing "B", a bouncing "B", a bouncing "B." Baby has a bouncing "B" that makes a sound like this-- /b/.

Tune to: **"The Farmer in the Dell"**
Song: **"Baby Bear's in Bed"**
(Whisper the song in the room or walking down the hall.)

Baby bear's in bed.
Baby bear's in bed.
Let's be very quiet.
For baby bear's in bed!

Sing "Blues for the letter 'B'" from the "More Natural Learning Songs from A-Z" cassette.

Fingerplay:

Baby Bears

Five baby bears in the bed,	(Hold up five fingers.)
One rolled over and hit his head.	(Hands on head.)
Four baby bears in the bed,	(Hold up four fingers.)
One left to go and eat some bread.	(Pretend to eat.)
Three baby bears in the bed,	(Three fingers.)
"I've got to go," one baby bear said.	(Put hands on face.)
Two baby bears in the bed,	(Hold up two fingers.)
I want my pajamas that are red!	(Put hands on hips.)
One baby bear in the bed,	(Hold up one finger.)
He's so comfortable with the	(Put both hands on side of face
whole bedspread.	and pretend to go to sleep.)

Fingerplay:

Baby Bunny

Baby bunny dressed in blue.
(Hold up two fingers on one hand like bunny ears)
Met another; then there were two.
(Use two hands and hold up index and middle fingers.)
Bouncy bunnies to the left.
(Move fingers to left.)
Bouncy bunnies to the right.
(Move fingers to right.)
Bouncy bunnies get in bed.
(One bunny bounces to your back.)
Off to bed, you sleepy heads.
(Bounce other bunny to the back.)

Motion Poem

Baby bunny bounces high;   (Jump high.)
Baby bunny bounces low;   (jump low.)
Baby bunny blinks his eyes;   (Blink eyes.)
Baby Bunny waves good-bye.   (Wave good-bye.)

Always acknowledge children whose first or last name begins with letter that you are emphasizing.

NOTES:

Letter C Investigations:

- **Learn how caterpillars make cocoons.**
- **Learn about catfish.**
- **Learn about the cat family.**
- **Learn about clowns.**
- **Learn how crocodiles are different from alligators.**
- **Learn about colors.**
- **Learn about corn.**
- **Learn about a cactus.**
- **Learn about cotton.**

> To purchase a school kit to learn about cotton, send $9.50 to:
> Little Bales of Cotton
> P.O. Box 305
> Stoneville, Ms 38776

- **Learn about The Coca-Cola Company.**

> Send for an information packet to:
> Coca-Cola USA
> Consumer Information Center
> P.O. Drawer 1734
> Atlanta, GA 30301

Art:

⇒ Draw clowns in a car.

⇒ Color on cardboard.

⇒ Paint with a corn cob.

⇒ Draw or paint a calico cat.

⇒ Discover colors. Take heavy-duty paper towels, twist from middle, dip point into colored water (yellow) then into (red).

⇒ Cut up colored transparencies. (red, yellow, blue, green) Put part of one over another to discover new colors.

⇒ Make a fun instamatic camera. Cut a small piece of cardboard about 4"x5". Hot glue a black 35 mm film holder on the cardboard, decorate the camera with buttons and pieces of construction paper, and tie a string to hang the camera around the neck. On back glue rectangular piece of paper on three sides. Cut pictures out of a magazine or draw pictures of words with /k/ sound. Have one picture that's a clown to have fun with someone. Take a walk outside, take pictures of anything. Let children discover the sites outside and encourage them to tell when they take a picture of a <u>C</u> word with the /k/ sound. Remember to tell the children to say CLICK when taking a picture. (The children may discover there is a "K" at the end of "click." Remember the purpose is for the children to develop phonemic awareness for the hard sound of letter "C.")

Tactile:
*   Draw letter "C" on a piece of cardboard. Let children trace with glue and then sprinkle coffee or cornmeal on the "C."

Cooking: (Call it "cooking" instead of "baking" for letter "C.")
◊   Let the class cook cookies.
◊   Cook cupcakes and let children decorate the cupcakes with candy corn and put a candle in the middle.
◊   Cook cornbread.
◊   Cook corn on the cob. (Wash cobs and paint with them.)

Counting:
♥   Count carrot slices.
♥   Count Coca-Cola cans.
♥   Count and sort different coins.
♥   Incorporate few and many concept.
♥   Count crayons. (See crayons on p. 152)

Games:

- Play familiar card games.
- Sit in a circle and let one or more persons in the middle be "It." Let one person in the circle hold a card with the letter "C" on it. Instruct the other children to pretend to cough randomly. Only the person holding the letter "C" does not cough. "It" must find the person who is holding the letter "C."
- Pretend to be caterpillars and crawl on the floor. Curl up in a ball to pretend you are in a cocoon. Then wake up and spread arms to pretend to be a butterfly.

Fieldtrips and Special Days:

- ➢ Visit a cafeteria.
- ➢ Visit a farm that grows cotton or corn.
- ➢ Contact your local Coca-Cola Company to see if fieldtrips are available.
- ➢ Investigate and look for fieldtrips that are available in your area.
- ➢ Have someone dress up as a clown to visit your room.

Books:

Count on Calico Cat by Donald Charles
C is for Clown by Stan and Jan Berenstain
A Real Class Clown by "Otto Coontz
Counting Carnival by Feenie Ziner

Songs:

Tune to: **"The Farmer in the Dell"**
Song: **"Call The Letter "C""**
(When you call for the letter "C", cup your hands around your mouth.)

Call the letter "C" --/k/
Call the letter "C" --/k/
Call the letter "C" and Clap, Clap, Clap. (Clap with hands.)

Crocodile **(Put hands together at wrist and open and close them like a crocodile's mouth. Open and shut them with chant.)**
Crocodile, crocodile, cut your cake.
Crocodile, crocodile, jump in the lake.
Crocodile, crocodile, just be cool.
Crocodile, crocodile, stay in school.

Tune to: "**Are you Sleeping?**"
Song: "**Candy "C"**

Cotton candy, cake and cookies, caramel, caramel
Candy corn and cupcakes, candy corn and cupcakes,
Letter "C"-- /k/,/k/,/k/.

Clean your teeth, clean your teeth.
Carefully, Carefully.
A cavity is growing, a cavity is growing.
Clean them quick, clean them quick!

Fingerplay:

There was a little caterpillar crawling all about.
He worked and he worked without a doubt.
(Index finger wiggling)

Wrapping himself in a snug cocoon.
Waiting and waiting, will it be soon?
(Cover index finger with other hand.)

Look, he's coming out, my oh my!
For now he's become a beautiful butterfly.
(Cross thumbs and let fingers be fingers be butterfly wings.)

Always acknowledge children whose first or last name begins with letter that you are emphasizing.

NOTES:

Letter D Investigations:

- **Learn about doctors.**
- **Learn about dinosaurs.**
- **Learn about dentist.**
- **Learn about a dictionary.**
- **Learn about ducks.**
- **Learn about dogs.**

Art:

⇒ Draw a dog (or draw your dog) and tell about it.

⇒ Make dinosaur eggs with playdough.

⇒ Make playdough (recipe on p. 137)

⇒ Draw Donuts. (Learn about circles.)

⇒ Draw a picture about a dream.

⇒ Cut out dog in art section and fold ear down. (p.150)

Tactile:

∗ Draw letter "Dd" on paper. Let children trace with glue. (Make sure that children start in correct place. Let children sprinkle dirt on D's. (Dirty "D's)

Baking:

◊ Make donuts. (Use canned biscuits and cut hole in center.) Bake and sprinkle powdered sugar or cinnamon and sugar on top.

◊ Make edible playdough.

◊ Make Dreamy Desert. (recipe on p. 138)

Counting:

♥ Play dominoes and match dots.

♥ Make cards with numbers and corresponding dots. (Match)

♥ Count dinosaur eggs. (Use playdough or construction paper.)

♥ Count donuts on a dish. (Glue different amounts of donuts shapes on paper plate.)

Games:
- Pin the Tail on the Donkey
- Duck, Duck, Goose
- Dominoes
- Don't Do the Dishes (Let children sit in a circle and one child be "It" in the middle.) Pass out paper plates with different shapes or letters. Have several plates decorated with the Letter "D" on it. Place the paper plates face down in front of the children. Each child will turn over his/her dish. If they do not have the "D" dish, they will say "Don't Do the Dishes." When a child discovers the decorated "D" dish, he/she shouts "Diddle-Diddle-Dee" and runs around the circle back to his/her place. "It" must run to outer circle through runner's place and try to catch the runner. Next turn, runner is "It" and other child sits in the circle. You may pass out new dishes to children or continue with next person in circle if you have made several "D" plates. Don't Do the Dishes may be played in classroom. Let children sit in circle. Children can still turn plates over and say "Don't do the Dishes" or "Diddle-Diddle-Dee" throughout the circle. Then the children can pass the plates one move to the left and quickly let the children say the appropriate saying.
- Dancing Round the Letter "D." Children join hands and walk in one direction as they sing Dancing Round the Letter "D" song. Place an object that begins with /d/ sound or the letter "D" on a piece of paper. On the second verse, the children can squat down like ducks, sing song, and go around the "D." On the third verse, the children can pretend that they are digging as they go around the letter "D."

Fieldtrips and Special Days:
- ➢ Visit a doctor's office.
- ➢ Visit a dentist's office.
- ➢ Visit a donut shop.
- ➢ Invite dads to come and read a story to the class.

Books:

> The Fisher-Price Picture Dictionary   ISBN 0-87135-0
> Dinosaur Do's and Don'ts by Sydney Hoff
> Dreams by Ezra Jack Keats
> Dinny and Danny by Louis Slobodkin

Songs:

> **Tune to:**   **"Here We Go Round the Mulberry Bush"**
> **Song:**   **"Dancing Round the Letter "D"**

Dancing round the letter "D", the letter "D", the letter "D",
Dancing round the letter "D", diddle, diddle, "D" (/d/ sound optional at
end of song.)

> **Tune to:**   **"Mary Had a Little Lamb"**
> **Song:**   **"Dig in Dirt"**

Danny likes to dig in dirt, dig in dirt, dig in dirt.
Danny likes to dig in dirt because he is a dog.

> **Tune to:**   **"Jimmy Crack Corn"**
> **Song:**   **"Doctor or Dentist"**

Did you go to the dentist today?
Did you go to the doctor today?
Which one made you feel OK?
(teacher sings/speaks last line) If you had a cold.
(Children respond with "doctor" or "dentist.")

Substitute:
> If you had a cavity
> If you broke your leg
> If you chipped a tooth
> If you got your teeth cleaned
> If you have the flu

Tune to: **"He's Got the Whole World in His Hands"**
Song: **"Ducky Dip"**

Danny the duck likes to dips-si-do.	(One hand dips down.)
Diane the duck likes to dips-si-do.	(Other hand dips down.)
They both like to dips-si-do,	(Both hands dip down.)
But not in December.	(Hands wave to show no.)

Fingerplay:

Ten little doggies went out one day	(10 fingers up)
To dig in the dirt and play, play, play.	(Pretend to dig.)
Five were spotted, and five were not,	(Show one hand at a time.)
and at dinner time they ate a lot!	(Pretend to eat.)

Poem:

My Donut

I have a donut for my desert.
Oops, I dropped it in the dirt.
My dog discovered it was there
and ate it up to my despair.

Always acknowledge children whose first or last name begins with letter that you are emphasizing.

NOTES:

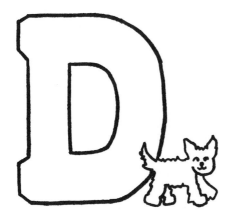

Letter E Investigations:

- **Learn about Mt. Everest.**
- **Learn about elephants.**
- **Learn about echoes.**
- **Learn about Eskimos.**
- **Learn about exercising.**
- **Learn about eggs.**

Art:

⇒ Cooperative art: Take large sheets of paper and paint a large mountain as Mt. Everest. For fun draw an elephant on the top to emphasize the letter "E."

⇒ Take a tack and punch a hole in two opposite sides of an egg. Blow through one hole to force egg to come out other end. Paint the eggs.

⇒ Make paper mache eggs. Blow up small oval balloons and paper mache them. Let dry and paint. Cut a hole and make into a bank.

⇒ Make elephant puppet. (See art section p. 151)

Tactile:

* Crush egg shells; wash and dry with paper towel. Mix small amount of food coloring and rubbing alcohol together. Mix together in plastic bag, drain, and let shells dry. Draw "Ee" on paper. Let children trace letters with glue and sprinkle egg shells on the letters.

Baking:

◊ Boil eggs and eat them.

◊ Make large sugar cookies in shape of an elephant's ear. (Make extras for the other teachers.)

Counting:

♥ Cut out egg shapes in groups of eggs or individual eggs. Children can count eggs or match dots on one egg to number on the corresponding egg.

♥ Count elbows in the class.

Games:

- Pretend to be elephants and let one arm hang down from nose.
- Egg on my Elbow. Cut out egg shape using poster paper. Children can have a relay race. Divide class in small equal groups. Children place egg on their elbow and walk to specific spot and return. Next child will take the egg and place on his/her elbow.
- Go to the End. Have children stand in a row facing the teacher. The teacher will have children's names on individual cards. When teacher holds up a name, that child must "Go to the End." When he/she gets there, child says, "I am at the end." May incorporate "front" in game. Another teacher can hold cards with children's names, and when she holds up a child's name, that child must come to the front. Children must watch carefully as their name may be called out for either direction quickly.

Fieldtrips and Special Days:

- ➤ Pretend to go on a safari and look for elephants.
- ➤ Visit a classroom in an elementary school.
- ➤ Take a ride on an elevator.

Books:

Ethel's Exceptional Egg by Linda Bourke

The Ant and the Elephant, Ella by Bill Peet

The Story of Babar, the Little Elephant by Jean de Brunhoff

Meg's Eggs by Helen Nicoll

Songs:

Tune to:	**"Mary Had a Little Lamb"**
Song:	**"Ellie the Elephant"**

Ellie had an elephant, elephant, elephant.

Ellie had an elephant; It made a sound like this--/e/, /e/, /e/.

  (May use Edward for the second verse)

Tune to: "Are You Sleeping?"
Song: "Echo"
Teacher sings first, and children echo.

Be my echo,	Be my echo,
Letter E,	Letter E,
Be my echo,	Be my echo,
/e/, /e/, /e/.	/e/, /e/, /e/.

Song may be used with other letters and sounds.
Song may be used to say one word in English and then the second word in another language.

Be my echo,	Be my echo,
Agua,	Agua,
Be my echo,	Be my echo,
Water,	Water .

Sing "Extra, Extra" from the "32 Natural Learning Songs from A-Z" cassette.

Fingerplay:

A circus elephant I went to see.
(Hold hand over eyes.)

He had 4 legs and was bigger than me.
(Hold up 4 fingers and point to self.)

He had two ears big and round.
(Show two fingers and make a circle with hands.)

And one long nose that made a sound.   /eeeeeeeeeeeeeeeee/
(Put arm like trunk and make elephant noise.)

28

Fingerplay:
Ethel was a hen who laid 10 eggs.
(Hold up 10 fingers.)

Each chick hatched and had two legs.
(Cup hands together and open, pointing both index fingers upward.)

They would play and have their fun.
(Wiggle all 10 fingers.)

But when Ethel called, they would come!
(While wiggling fingers, clasp hands together.)

(Ask: How many legs did 10 chicks have?
Let children draw 10 chicks to find out.)

Fingerplay:
On the first, Evelyn was sent
(Hold up index finger.)

To pay Mr. Edward the apartment rent.
(Hold out palm as to pay money.)

On the elevator, Evelyn went
(Point right index finger upward and sit on palm of other hand.)

And did her job excellent!
(Clap hands.)

Always acknowledge children whose first or last name begins with letter that you are emphasizing.

NOTES:

Letter F Investigations:

- **Learn about frogs.**
- **Learn about flags.**
- **Learn about fingerprints.**
- **Learn about fish.**
- **Learn about flowers.**
- **Learn about firemen.**

Art:

⇒ Let each child design a fancy fish. Have a table with shiny things that they can use. Let each child tell about their fancy fish.

⇒ Let each child design their own family flag. Staple a rectangular piece of paper to a straw. The only instruction, if any, is to use the correct number of stars to represent the number of family members. Teacher supplies shiny stars.

⇒ Let class design a class or kindergarten flag.

⇒ Draw funny faces.

⇒ Use large sheet of paper and paint with feet. Place sheet on wall outside room. In large print write "Follow these Feet to Fun."

⇒ Draw a picture of a friend and tell why that person (or persons) is your friend(s).

⇒ Put your fingerprints on paper.

Tactile:

* Finger-paint "F's."

* Arrange French fries to form "F."

* Make a frosting "F." (Make frosting and put in a tube or small plastic bag. Cut tiny hole and let children squeeze frosting on "F.")

Baking:

◊ Bake French fries. (Emphasize that they were frozen at first.)

◊ Make a fruit salad.

◊ Make frosting for "Frosting F."

◊ Make a Fabric "F."

31

Counting:

- ♥ Count the fancy fish.
- ♥ Count in order: First, Second, Third, Fourth, Fifth (May make cards with numbers 1-5 on them. Let children arrange themselves in order, and then let each child say the order that they are in.)
- ♥ Count fingers on each hand.

Games:

- Freeze Tag
- The Farmer in the Dell
- Card game: Go Fish
- Make a fish game with fish shapes and magnets. In 30 seconds, see how many fish you can catch. You can have children draw a card from a stack with a picture of a fish on it. The children must fish to match their fish card. Children must throw back ones that do not match. May be used with opposites, numbers, and corresponding dots.

Fieldtrips and Special Days:

- ➢ Visit a farm.
- ➢ Visit a factory.
- ➢ Go Fishing with the fish game.
- ➢ Fabulous Friday (Fingerpaint, paint with feet, eat French fries, etc.)
- ➢ Visit a florist.

Books:

Faces Faces by Barbara Brenner

Fairy Tales and Fables by Eve Morel

Farm Numbers 1,2,3 by Donald Smith

Father Fox's Pennyrhymes by Clyde Walson

Fee Fi Fo Fum by Raymond Buggs

Songs:

Tune to: **"Mary Had a Little Lamb"**

Song: **"Funny Frog"**

The farmer found a funny frog, funny frog, funny frog.

The farmer found a funny frog that followed him around.

(Let someone be the farmer and let the farmer tap another child to be the frog to hop in the center of a circle. Then the frog becomes the farmer.)

Tune to: "He's Got the Whole World in His Hands"
Song: "F" For Family"

I've found the letter "F" for Family.
I've found the letter "F" for Family.
I've found the letter "F" for Family.
Fee Fi Family!
(May substitute other words: funny, friendly, fireman, finger)

Tune to: "Baa, Baa, Black Sheep"
Song: "Freddy Freckles"

Freddy Freckles is four years old.
In February, he'll turn five.
He lives on a farm in Florida.
He goes fishing for flounder.
Freddy Freckles is four years old.
In February, he'll turn five.

Fingerplay:

I have five fingers on each hand.
(Show each hand.)

I like to put them in the sand.
(Wiggle all fingers.)

When I hide my thumb just so,
(Bend thumbs back.)

There's only four that I can show.
(Show four fingers on each hand.)

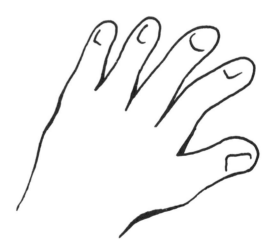

Always acknowledge children whose first or last name begins with letter that you are emphasizing.

NOTES:

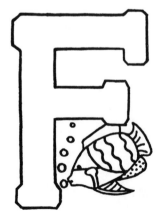

Letter G Investigations:

- **Learn about gourds.**
- **Learn about grapes.**
- **Learn about grasshoppers.**
- **Learn about gardens.**
- **Learn about glasses.**
- **Learn about gazelles.**
- **Learn about gorillas.**
- **Learn about geese.**
  (A father goose is called a gander and a baby goose is called a gosling.)

Art:

⇒ Paint or draw a cluster of grapes.

⇒ Paint with a golf ball. Put paper and puddles of paint in box and let ball roll around.

⇒ Draw the shape of your hand and draw a glove on it.

⇒ Draw or paint a picture of the goose that laid the golden egg after you have read Jack and the Beanstalk. Use gold glitter for the egg.

Tactile:

* Write Letter "Gg" on paper. Mix green paint and glue together in glue bottle. Guide children to trace letter with green glue.

* Golden "G"   Write letter "Gg" on paper. Let children apply glue and sprinkle gold glitter. (Could use green glitter.)

Baking:

◊ Make green cookies. (Add green food color to dough.)

◊ Make a gallon of green Kool-aid

◊ Eat green grapes.

◊ Make ghost cookies. Use sugar cookie recipe and put two chocolate chips for the eyes.

Counting:

- ♥ Count golden eggs.
- ♥ Count gold fish.
- ♥ Count grapes.
- ♥ Guess how many grapes are in a small glass. (Let children guess and all count the grapes together.)
- ♥ Count grasshoppers in the green grass. Make pictures of grasshoppers in the green grass. Make each picture with different amounts of grasshoppers. Let children count grasshoppers.
- ♥ Count and sort gloves. (Collect different colors and styles of gloves.)

Games:

- • Gathering Grapes: Let children reach in a box to gather 5 grape shapes. Teacher has beforehand marked the grapes with different shapes and colors. If a child finds two that match he/she may keep the pair and put the rest back in the box for the next person.
- • Go Tell Grandma and Grandpa, the Geese are Gone! Choose two to be Grandma and Grandpa and one child to be the grandchild. Other children will be the geese. Grandma and Grandpa stand together and grandchild runs to tell them "Grandma, Grandpa, the Geese are gone." Then Grandma and Grandpa and grandchild gather the geese until only one goose is left. Then start game over. When geese are captured or touched, they must stay in one place until end of game.

Fieldtrips and Special Days:

- ➢ Visit a garden.
- ➢ Visit a grape orchard.
- ➢ Invite a grandmother and/or a grandfather to come and read a story.
- ➢ Have a green Day. (Everyone wear something green.)

Books:

A Gaggle of Geese by Eve Merriam

Gobble Growl Grunt by Peter Spier

Gone is my Goose by Dorothy Clarke Kock

Green Says Go by Edward Randolph Emberley

Gordon, the Goat by Munro Leaf

Songs:
>**Tune to:**   **"London Bridge"**
>**Song:**   **"Get Your Glasses"**

Grandma, get your glasses, glasses, glasses.
Grandma, get your glasses and see the letter "G."
(In first verse, let child or children put on plastic sunglasses which have
had the lens taken out.

Grandma, get the letter "G", letter "G", letter "G."
Grandma, get the letter "G" and then sit down.
(In second verse, let child or children go to center to find the letter "G"
with many other letters of the alphabet or find a picture which begins
with /g/ sound.)

(When singing the song the second time, choose boys and insert
Grandpa where Grandma is used.)

>**Tune to:**   **"Twinkle, Twinkle Little Star"**
>**Song:**   **"Goodness Gracious"**

Girls and guys, wave good-bye.
Goodness gracious, great and good.

Gorillas and grasshoppers, green green grass.
Gifts for a goat-- /g/,/g/,/g/.

Girls and guys, wave good-bye.
Goodness gracious, great and good.

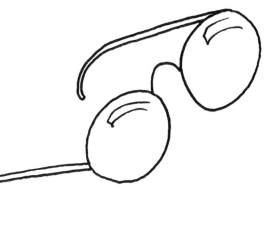

Poem:
Giddy Up

Giddy up, giddy up, giddy up, and go, go, go!
Giddy up, giddy up, giddy up, and don't be slow!

I'm going to my Grandma's; she's waiting there for me,
And soon I'll have some goodies sitting on her knee.

Giddy up, giddy up, giddy up, and go, go, go!
Giddy up, giddy up, giddy up, and don't be slow!

(Vocabulary word that means to ride fast on a horse.....Gallop)

Fingerplay:
Green Grapes

Five green grapes growing on a vine.   (Hold up five fingers.)
I picked one 'cause it looked so fine!   (Touch thumb and fold it down.)

Four green grapes growing on a vine.   (Hold up four fingers.)
I picked another for my Valentine!   (Touch index finger & fold down.)

Three green grapes growing on a vine.   (Hold up three fingers.)
I ate another, I couldn't decline!   (Touch middle finger and fold down.)

Two green grapes growing on a vine.   (Hold two fingers up.)
I ate another in the sunshine.   (Touch ring finger and fold down.)

One green grape growing on a vine.   (Hold up little finger.)
I ate it too, cause they were all mine!   (Fold down little finger.)

Always acknowledge children whose first or last name begins with letter that you are emphasizing.

NOTES:

Letter H Investigations:

- **Learn about hibernation.**
- **Learn about hippos.**
- **Learn about good health.**
- **Learn about your heart.**
- **Learn about hats.**
- **Learn about helicopters.**
- **Learn about horses.**
- **Learn about hobbies.**
- **Learn about honeybees.**
- **Learn about hummingbirds.**

Art:

⇒ Do hand casting in plaster of Paris.

⇒ Make paper hats decorated with hearts. Make traditional triangular hats or make Happy Hats. Place 3 to 4 pieces on top of each other but not directly in line with other pages of newspaper. Have someone hold their hand directly on the sheets which have been placed on child's head. Wrap masking tape twice around newspapers on child's head. (Follow the hair line.) Fold back edges and tape with masking tape. Make a brim for boys and place a colorful napkin on top of the girls' hats. Let children decorate them at the art center. (Old silk or plastic flowers, and Mardi Gras necklaces make the hats so cute.) For a baseball cap, remove papers from child's head and cut ¾'s of newspaper off by the masking tape. Fold remaining edge or newspaper to form brim.

⇒ Let children draw steps to "How to Cook a Hotdog."

⇒ Let children trace their hands. Let children decorate with jewelry. Hang pictures on the wall. Let children tell "How our Hands Help Us."

⇒ Let the children paint pictures of high heels.

⇒ Let the children cut out the high heel in the art section and then write "H" on the inside. (Cut out high heel on p. 154)

Tactile:

* Make Hairy "H's." Draw an "H" with a marker. Let children apply glue and bits of yarn.

* On an "H" let children apply glue and then bits of hay.

* On an 8x11½ piece of paper let children draw a "huge" uppercase "H" and then design a hat on the "H." Be sure to define the word "huge."

* Make Honeycomb cereal "H's." Glue pieces of Honeycomb cereal to letter "H."

Baking:

◊ Cook hotdogs.

◊ Make heart shaped cookies.

◊ Make Honeybutter (Recipe on p. 138)

Counting:

♥ Count how many hands two people have. (three people, four people, etc.)

♥ Ask each child whether they like hotdogs or hamburgers best. Graph the outcome. (Graph chart on p. 158)

♥ Have a box with hearts in it. On each heart write a number to 10 and the dots that correspond. Let each child pick a heart and hop the amount of times his heart says.

♥ Graph hair color in the classroom. (Graph chart on p. 158)

♥ Cut things in half.

♥ Learn about high and low.

Games:

• Hula Hoop Contest

• Hula Hoop instruction: Cut a string 7 ½ to 8 feet long. Purchase ¾ " polyurethane black hose. (May be bought in 100 ft. rolls at hardware store) Mark off lengths of 7 ½ to 8 feet pieces. Cut with small hand saw. Hold ends over source of heat for about 10 to 20 seconds to warm tube ends. Insert ¾ " connector bought at hardware store to join ends of hula-hoop.

- Honeybee, Find Your Home: Cut out squares of paper and glue or draw pictures with /h/ sound and other pictures of letter sounds on the square cards. Paste a bee hive with letter "H" on the back of the /h/ pictures. (See Below) Take a large cardboard box and cut out entrance and exit for honeybees to enter and exit and then go to their seat. On the front of the box, put the word "Hive." Also, in front of the box place a silk flower for honeybees to touch before going into hive. Place the hive in the center of the circle. Let children sit in a circle and pretend to be honeybees. Explain that honeybees must collect nectar from flowers to make honey. In their hive they turn the nectar into honey. With the children in the circle or standing by their seat, hold up a card for each child. Let each child say the picture on the card and identify (yes or no) whether the picture has the /h/ sound. Teacher will turn picture over. If the hive is on the back, the child may go to the hive. If not, the child must remain in the circle. When the child goes to the hive, let him/her touch the flower and enter and exit the hive, then return to place in circle. Keep going around the circle fairly quickly using the cards over and over. Instruct them to hum softly as they go to the hive, and they must stop when they exit. Go around the circle several times as to let all children go through the hive.

Fieldtrips and Special Days:
➢ Visit a hospital.
➢ Pretend to go into hibernation.
➢ Hat Day: Let children wear a hat to school or make hats to wear.
➢ Have a Hula Hoop contest.

Books:
How Hippo by Marcia Brown
The Horse in Harry's Room by Sidney Hoff
Alfred goes House Hunting by Bill Binzen
The Cat in the Hat by Theordor Suess Geisel

Songs:

    Tune to: **"The Farmer in the Dell"**
    Song: **"Hello"**

I want to say Hello. (Wave)
I want to say Hello. (Wave)

Hi Ho I'm glad you're here;
I want to say Hello. (Wave)

    Tune to: **"Jimmy Crack Corn"**
    Song: **"I Am Very Happy"**
My hair and my heel are part of me.
(Touch those parts.)

My heart and my head are part of me.
(Touch those parts.)

I hear with ears and hold my hand.
(Touch ears then lock hands together.)

I am very happy.
(Smile)

Fingerplay:

Five humming birds flying in the air
(Hold up five fingers.)

The first one landed in my hair.
(Touch thumb.)

The second and third were a pair.
(Touch index and middle finger and let these fingers come together.)

The fourth humming bird didn't care.
(Touch ring finger.)

The fifth humming bird hummed everywhere.
(Touch little finger and hum.)

Motion Poem:

I hop on my horse and go to town.	(Pretend to ride horse.)
I ride up high and I don't fall down.	(Place arms high and then low.)
I wear a hat so my hair won't blow.	(Put hand on head.)
and when I want to stop, I just say Ho!	(Pull back on reins.)

Always acknowledge children whose first or last name begins with letter that you are emphasizing.

NOTES:

Letter I Investigations:

- **Learn about Insects.**
- **Learn about iguanas.**
- **Learn about Indians.**
- **Learn about igloos.**
- **Learn about an inch.**
- **Learn about Italy.**

Art:

⇒ Make igloos. Collect cool whip containers and small paper cups. Cut small circle on side of container. Insert small paper cup into opening, letting the opening of cup jut out for entrance of igloo. Place container and cup on piece of cardboard. (Optional: Glue container to board the night before.) Cover container and cup with whipped mixture. (Beat together 2 parts of Ivory soap to one part of water.) Cut out "I" to place on top of igloo.

⇒ Let children paint their initials.

⇒ Draw or paint Indian symbols.

⇒ Paint inchworms.

⇒ Draw or paint insects. (Remember six legs.)

Tactile:

∗ Make the Letter "I" using one inch squares.

Baking:

◊ Make initial cookies. Use sugar cookie mix and let children paint one of their initials on a cookie with small paint brush and food coloring; then bake.

◊ Make instant pudding.

Counting:

- ♥ Measure using inches. How many inches is your finger? a car? a block? a crayon?
- ♥ Count how many legs an insect has.
- ♥ Count the one inch squares that were used in the Tactile Letter "I."
- ♥ Count inchworms that you have placed in the room.
- ♥ Count inchworms that are inside a book or outside of the book.

Games:

- • Pretend to be an inchworm.
- • Use imagination to make up a story.
- • Imitate an insect.
- • Hold up cards with each child's initials. When the child recognizes his/her initials, he/she may stand.

Fieldtrips and Special Days:

- ➢ Use imagination and go to Italy or anywhere.
- ➢ Have a Native American visit the classroom.

Books:

Inch by Inch by Leo Lionni
If I were a Cricket by Kazue Mizumura

Songs:

Tune to: **"Twinkle, Twinkle Little Star"**
Song: **"Inchworm"**

Inchworm, inchworm, how are you?
Here's an Indian in an igloo.

Insects flying way up high,
The letter "I" says-- /i/, /i/, /i/

Inchworm, inchworm, how are you?
Here's an Indian in an igloo.

Tune to: "Itsy Bitsy Spider"
Song: "Itsy Bitsy Insect"

The itsy bitsy insect went inside the igloo.   (Walk two fingers up the arm.)

It bit the iguana, and he began to itch!   (Scratch the top of arm.)

Out came the insecticide which made the insect ill,
So the itsy bitsy insect inched out of the igloo.
                    (Walk very slowly down the arm with the two fingers.)

Sing "Imagine an Iguana" from the "32 Natural Learning Songs from A-Z" cassette.

Fingerplay:
5 inchworms inching up a tree,
(Wiggle five fingers.)

5 insects invited them to see
(Hold up other hand.)

An Iguana inside the tree.
(Place hand inside other hand.)

Use your imagination and you will see
(Point index finger to head.)

All 10 having fun in a tree!
(Wiggle all 10 fingers.)

Always acknowledge children whose first or last name begins with letter that you are emphasizing.

NOTES:

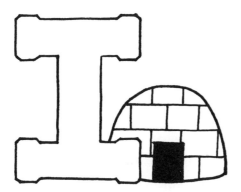

Letter J Investigations:

- **Learn about Japan.**
- **Learn about jaguars.**
- **Learn about jackrabbits.**
- **Learn about jets.**
- **Learn about jellyfish.**
- **Learn about a jungle.**
- **Learn about Jupiter.**

Art:

⇒ Make Japanese flags. (white background with red circle in middle)

⇒ Make a jigsaw puzzle. Color pictures of joy on stiff paper. On back draw lines vertical and horizontal and cut into pieces.

⇒ Design a piece of jewelry or draw a picture with jewelry in it.

⇒ Make a mural of Jack and the Bean Stalk.

⇒ Draw a picture of a jungle.

⇒ Draw a jelly jar and color or paint the flavor of jelly.

Tactile:

* Glue jelly beans on letter "J" or draw jelly beans to make a "J."

* Let children trace a jumbo "J" on stiff paper. (See Jumbo "J" on p. 53) Let children cut into large pieces for "Jigsaw "J."

Counting:

♥ Count and sort Jelly Beans.(either real or cut out with construction paper.)

♥ Graph the favorite flavor of jellybeans for the class.

♥ Jump rope and count how many times each person can jump.

Games:

- Jump Rope
- Listen to first verse of *Jump* by the Pointer sisters. Jump when you hear the word "jump." While listening to the song, jog in place, pretend to juggle (up high or down low), jumping jacks, and jump in place.

- Jack and Jenny in the Jellybean Jar: Cut out construction paper jelly beans and put in jar. Let children secretly pull out one jellybean. Use only Green, Red, Yellow, and Black. Choose a boy and a girl to be Jack and Jenny. Tell and illustrate to the children that there are only four colors. Children may sit in circle or in their seats. Let Jack and Jenny go to one child at a time. They must guess the color of the jelly bean in ONE guess. If they are incorrect, the child nods no and they go to the next person. (Children may learn by elimination what colors to guess.) If they are correct, the child jumps twice, and he/she becomes Jack or Jenny. (He/she may put jellybean back in the jar and the previous Jack or Jenny must go and draw their jellybean.) Jack and Jenny alternate turns.

Fieldtrips and Special Days:
➤ Visit a Judge at his job.
➤ Have person of Japanese descent visit the classroom. If this person can write characters in Japanese, he/she may write each child's name in Japanese or just write some Japanese characters.
➤ Tell a joke day. Let children tell jokes to the class. Read a joke book to the class.

Books:
Hester the Jester by Ben Shecter
The Judge by Harve Zemach
Jack and the Bean Stalk

Songs:
Tune to: **"Are You Sleeping"**
Song: **"J" Song"**

Can you jog, can you jog, in one place, in one place? Pretend to juggle, pretend to juggle, and then jump, and then jump.

Sing "Jazzy "J" from the "32 Natural Learning Songs from A-Z" cassette.

Tune to: **"Did You Ever See a Lassie?"**
Song: **"Jump for "J"**

When you hear a "J" word, a "J" word, a "J" word,
When you hear a "J" word, jump up in the air.

In June or July, in jungles and Jamaica,
When you hear a "J" word, jump up in the air.

With Jack or with Jenny, with Judy or Johnny,
When you hear a "J" word, jump up in the air.

Tune to: **"London Bridge is Falling Down"**
Song: **"Joyfully Jumping"**

Join the fun and jump for joy, jump for joy, jump for joy.
Join the fun and jump for joy, just where you are.

Join the fun and jump for joy, jump for joy, jump for joy.
Join the fun and jump for joy, just with a friend. (Join hands with friend.)

Fingerplay:

Jellybeans in the jar I see.   (Hold up 10 fingers.)
There're five for Jenny and five for me.   (Hold up each hand.)
We jump each time we put one in:
1 (jump) 2 (jump) 3 (jump) 4 (jump) 5 (jump)   **(REPEAT)**
(First boys jump 5 times then girls jump 5 times.)

Fingerplay:

5 jelly beans jumping in the den;   (Hold 5 fingers up.)
5 more joined and then there were 10.   (Show other hand.)
10 jelly beans jumping in the den,   (Show both hands.)
just joking around with great big grins.   (Smile.)

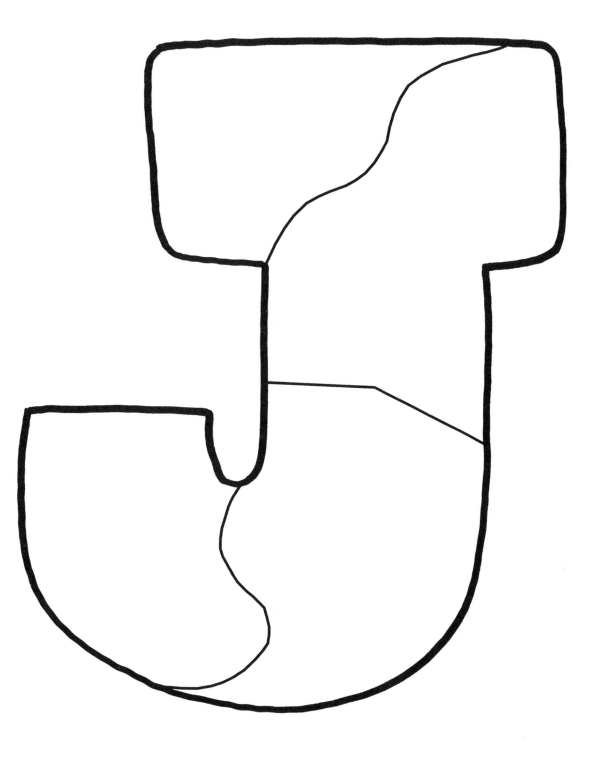

Always acknowledge children whose first or last name begins with letter that you are emphasizing. See if there are any Jr.'s

NOTES:

Letter K Investigations:

- **Learn about kangaroos.**
- **Learn about koalas.**
- **Learn about kites.**
- **Learn about a king.**
- **Learn about a kookaburra.**
- **Learn about a kaleidoscope.**
- **Learn about a kayak.**

Art:

⇒ Draw Kangaroos and their babies. (joeys)

⇒ Paint scenes with kites. Tell about your picture.

⇒ Let children trace keys or place keys between two sheets of paper and color on top to make prints of keys.

⇒ Draw a picture of someone being kind and tell about your picture.

⇒ Make crowns for kings in the class. (See art section p. 58)

Tactile:

* Write the Letter "Kk" on a piece of paper. Let children apply glue correctly as in writing the "Kk." Let children sprinkle Kellogg's Special K cereal on the glue.

* Let children paint with ketchup the Letter "Kk" or paint with red paint to symbolize ketchup.

* Put kidney beans on the Letter "Kk."

Baking:

◊ Cook kidney beans for a soup or chili.

◊ Let children sample a kumquat.

◊ Let children sample a kiwi.

Counting:

♥ Estimate the number of kidney beans in several small containers.

♥ Make a matching game with mother kangaroos and their babies, joeys. The joeys could have a number and the mother's corresponding dots. (See art section p. 152)

♥ For small groups: On several pieces of paper, trace 5 different keys. Put the keys that you have traced in the center of the children with the sheets of paper. As in a puzzle let the children match the keys to the traced keys on the sheets of paper.

♥ If you have access to old keys, hot glue different amounts of keys to sturdy pieces of cardboard. Let the children count the keys. Put the correct number of the keys on the back of the board.

Games:

- Pretend to be kangaroos and hop around the room.
- On white cards, with different markers draw uppercase "K's", and on other cards, draw matching lowercase "k's." Make some "Kk's" poka-dotted or striped to have a variety of matchings. Let children match the uppercase "K" to the lowercase "k." When a match is found the pair sit down.
- What would be the "Kind" thing to do? Make statements to the class and then ask, "What would be the "Kind" thing to do? Here are a few statements.
  1. **A new child comes to our classroom.**
  2. **John and Mike are arguing on the playground.**
  3. **Amanda and Nikie want to play with the same baby doll.**
  4. **Kate is sad because she isn't the leader today.**
  5. **Billy pushed Kendra while standing in line.**
  6. **The teacher is working with another child and you think about knocking the blocks over that Susie is playing with.**

Fieldtrips and Special Days:

➤ King and Queen Day: Explain that boys are called kings and girls are call queens. Let children make crowns and decorate them in the art center. Cut strips of construction paper to go around child's head. Glue crown on the strip and decorate. Let boys put glitter on the "K" for "king." Girls may decorate their crowns and their glitter "K" can stand for being "kind queen." (Crown shape on p. 58)

➤ Fly a kite.

➤ Visit a K-Mart. Find things that begin with /k/ sound.

➤ Emphasize kick ball on the playground.

Books:

Kangaroo and Kangaroo by Kathy Braun
Little New Kangaroo by Bernard Wiseman
Keep an Eye on Kevin by Genevieve Gray
Koala Lou by Mem Fox

Songs:

Tune to: **"Baa, Baa, Black Sheep"**
Song: **"K, K, Kindergarten"**

K, K, Kindergarten, Let's fly a kite.
Kelly's in the kitchen kissing a king.
K for my kitten and K for "keep"
and K for kindness --/k/, /k/, /k/.
Koalas and Kangaroos kicking to and fro
The Letter "K" I hope you know!

Tune to: **"London Bridge"**
Song: **"The King is in the Kitchen"**

The King is in his kitchen, kitchen, kitchen.
The King is in his kitchen playing a kazoo.
(Second verse: Eating a kumquat.)

Fingerplay:

5 baby kangaroos all in a row,
(Hold up 5 fingers.)

When they see their mother they kick just so.
(Let fingers thrust forward.)

For their mothers they have missed,
(Hold up other hand.)

So they run and give her a great big kiss.
(Wiggle right hand fingers toward left hand and touch fingertips.)

Rebus:

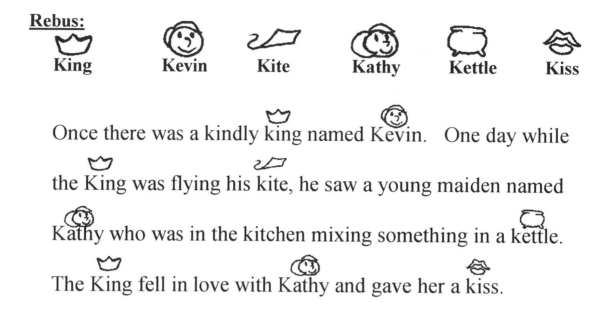

King   Kevin   Kite   Kathy   Kettle   Kiss

Once there was a kindly king named Kevin.   One day while

the King was flying his kite, he saw a young maiden named

Kathy who was in the kitchen mixing something in a kettle.

The King fell in love with Kathy and gave her a kiss.

Teacher may draw "K" or "Q" on crown.

Always acknowledge children whose first or last name begins with letter that you are emphasizing.

NOTES:

Letter L Investigations:

- **Learn about the library.**
- **Learn about lambs.**
- **Learn about lions.**
- **Learn about lobsters.**
- **Learn about lizards.**
- **Learn about leaves.**

Art:

⇒ Leaf drawings: Take different leaves and place on a table and cover with a sheet of paper. Hold paper very still and press against leaves. Color long strokes on the sheet of paper. Prints of the leaves will begin to show.

⇒ Draw a picture of "Mary had a Little Lamb" Sing the song first.

⇒ Draw or paint pictures of "love."

⇒ Paint with a lemons or limes.

⇒ On a white sheet of paper color a large section with a yellow crayon. On top of the yellow, color with a black crayon. With a toothpick, scratch to draw a house, apartment, or a building. Then scratch a small opening for windows, and the yellow light to show. Scratch a jagged line for lightening.

Tactile:

* Form Letter "Ll" out of homemade playdough. (p. 137) Let the dough dry and then paint lavender or yellow (for lemon) and sprinkle lemon flavoring on top.

* Draw large Letter "L" on a sturdy piece of paper. Let children glue small leaves or parts of leaves on the "L."

Baking:

◊ Make lemonade.

◊ Make lollipops.

◊ Make love cookies in a heart shape.

Counting:

- ♥ Sort leaves.
- ♥ Draw ladybugs with dots on their wings. Cut out large leaves that have numbers on them. Place the leaves on the floor and have the children place the corresponding ladybug on the leaf.
- ♥ Draw ladders with different amounts of rungs (steps). Put ladder in order from one rung to five rungs. Let children paint or color ladders with different amounts of rungs.
- ♥ Make a graph of the number of children who are left-handed and right-handed.
- ♥ Emphasize more and less.
- ♥ Give special notice to the last person in line!
- ♥ Take about loud and soft.

Games:

- Laughing Game: Let each child try to make someone laugh or (smile) with funny faces (cannot touch). If the person laughs or smiles, then that person is "It."
- Look for a Lizard: Make copies of the "L" shaped lizard. While the children are closing their eyes, place two lizards in sight in the room. Select a different four children each time to "Look for the Lizards." (Instruct the children not to run in the room.) When a child finds a lizard, he/she takes the lizard and sits down at his seat or in a circle.
- Line up Little Lambs: Cut out lamb shapes in five different colors. On the red lambs, put numbers one through five. On blue lambs put numbers one through five, etc. Divide the class in groups of five. Let each group sit together with their lambs on the floor and numbers facing down. When you say "Line up Little Lambs," the children must pick up a lamb and line up. (Game may be extended to 10 lambs.)

Fieldtrips and Special Days:
- ➤ Visit a library.
- ➤ Take a walk and pick up leaves.

Books:

I Like the Library by Anne F. Rockwell
The Good Llama by Anne R. Rockwell
The Sleepy Little Lion by Margaret Wise Brown

Songs:

Tune to:	**"Are You Sleeping"**
Song:	**"Letter "L""**

Letter "L", Letter "L", lemonade, lemonade;
Send a little letter, send a little letter--
I love you, I love you.

Tune to:	**"I'm a Little Teapot"**
Song:	**"Let's Go To Lunch"**

Let's go to lunch, you'll like it a lot.
Lick your lips, it's time for lunch.
Lasagna and lima beans, lemonade to drink,
Licorice for last; now don't be late.
Let's go to lunch, you'll like it a lot
Lick your lips, it's time for lunch!

Tune to:	**"Row, Row, Row Your Boat"**
Song:	**"La, La, La"**

La, La, La, La, La,
La, La, La, La, La,
La, La, La, La, La,
Lucy loves to laugh.

(On the second verse, change to "Larry Loves to Laugh.")
Girls stand and sing first verse, and boys stand and sing the second
verse. This song may be sung in a round. Also, it may be sung soft or
loud.

Poem:

Lots to Learn

I climb a ladder with both hands.
(Pretend to climb.)

I leap, and on both feet I land.
(Jump on word "leap.")

I listen, I laugh, and I look,
(Put hand to ear, to mouth, and to eyes.)

And I'm learning to read a book.
(Hold hands to form a book.)

Motion Poem:

Lean to the Left

Lean to the left and lean to the right.
(Lean to left and then to right.)

Stand up, sit down, look at the light.
(Follow directions & look at ceiling light.)

Lift your leg, the left I beg.
(Lift left leg.)

Lick a lollipop, and please don't stop.
(Pretend to lick a lollipop.)

(Second time around, do motions while pretending to lick a lollipop.)

Fingerplay:

Five lizards live on a log.
(Hold up five fingers and then cover palm with other hand.)

One left to live with a frog.
(Hold thumb of right hand down behind log.)

One left to live with a dog.
(Hold index finger down behind log.)

Two left to live with a hog.
(Hold middle and ring finger down.)

One little lizard living in the bog. (Bog means a wet, spongy ground)
(Show little finger.)

Is a little lonely living on a log.
(Hold index finger up and swing side to side.)

Always acknowledge children whose first or last name begins with letter that you are emphasizing.

NOTES:

Letter M Investigations:

- **Learn about magic.**
- **Learn about Mexico.**
- **Learn about Mississippi.**
- **Learn about The Mighty Mississippi River.**
- **Learn about milk.**
- **Learn about money.**
- **Learn about magnets.**
- **Learn about mammals.**
- **Learn about monkeys.**

Art:

⇒ Draw or paint pictures and tell about them:
"My Mom and Me"
"The Monster"
"The Man in the Moon"
"Me"

⇒ Make Mr. and Miss Mouse ears. (Mouse Pattern on p. 155) Cut a band to go around child's head. Glue Mouse ears on band. On pink insert to ears, let children trace with glue over upper-case and lower-case M's. Sprinkle glitter on glue.

⇒ Make mosaic pictures with different colors of construction paper.

⇒ Use magic markers.

⇒ Place pennies, nickels, and dimes on sheet of paper. Place another sheet on paper on top and let children rub crayons across the top and the money will show through.

⇒ Draw the Mighty Mississippi River on a very long sheet of newsprint.

Tactile:

* Arrange mini-marshmallows on sheet to form "M." Children may eat the marshmallows or then apply glue to make a mini-marshmallow "M."

* Trace an upper-case "M" with mustard in a squeeze mustard jar. Let dry.

Baking:
◊ Make muffins.
◊ Make milkshakes.

Counting:
♥ Count marshmallows.
♥ Count the months in the year and see how many months begin with /m/.
♥ Discuss few and many.
♥ Play with a magnet and graph items that attract or not.
♥ Sort animals which are mammals or non-mammals.
♥ Measure different things in the classroom.

Games:
• Play "Mother May I?"
• March to Music
• Musical chairs
• Play a fishing game with magnets and fish for a match. (color match, number match, opposite match, etc.)
• Play a matching game with cards. When child turns over two cards that match, he/she keeps the cards and has another turn to match. If incorrect match, it becomes the next child's turn.
• Place several small items on a tray. While children close their eyes, remove two or three items and let children try to remember and name the items that were removed.
• Place several /m/ items on a tray and place in view of all children. Cover tray and let children try to remember what is on the tray.

Fieldtrips and Special Days:
➤ Make believe you are in Mexico. (Learn some Spanish words.)
➤ Have a Mom come and read a story.
➤ Visit a military base.
➤ Learn some magic tricks.
➤ Go to the post office and learn what happens to a letter when it is mailed.

Books:

Mike Mulligan and His Steam Shovel by Virginia Burton
Marc the Magnificent by Sue Alexander
The Marvelous Merry-Go-Round by Jane Watson
The Monkey and the Crocodile by Paul Galdone
M and M's Brand Chocolate Candies Counting Board Book by Barbara
B. McGath

Songs:

Tune to:	**"Twinkle, Twinkle Little Star"**
Song:	**"Mary Made a Mess"**

Mary made a mess.
Mary made a mess.
Mixing her milk,
Mixing her milk.
Her Mother made her clean it up.
She mopped the floor, but she was mad-- /m/,/m/,/m/.

Tune to:	**"Are You Sleeping"**
Song:	**"Months of the Year"**

January, February, March and April, May, June, July,
August and September, October and November
and last is December and we start again.

Tune to:	**"Mary Had a Little Lamb"**
Song:	**"Mommy Makes Me Make My Bed"**

My mommy makes me make my bed, make my bed, make my bed.
My mommy makes me make my bed first thing on Monday morn.

I must put on my mittens, mittens, mittens.
I must put on my mittens in the winter months.

Miss Mary had a merry mouse, merry mouse, merry mouse.
Miss Mary had a merry mouse which marched around the mat.

Rap: I'm Proud of Me!

I am _____ and I go to school. (fill in name)
I am learning and I am cool!

I care about myself, my family, and friends.
They know on me they can depend!

I care about my home and community!
And the world's a better place,
With someone like ME!

Fingerplay:

Five merry mice were born in May.	(Show five fingers.)
The first one said, "In the Mud, let's play."	(Touch thumb.)
The second one said, "No way, Hosea"!	(Touch index.)
The third one said, "In the middle I must stay."	(Touch middle.)
The fourth one said, " I am mad today."	(Touch ring finger.)
The fifth one said, "Our Mom we must obey."	(Touch little finger.)

Always acknowledge children whose first or last name begins with letter that you are emphasizing.

NOTES:

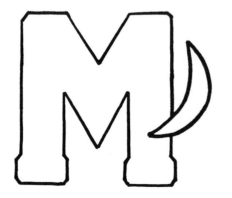

Letter N Investigations:

- **Learn about nests.**
- **Learn about names. (first, middle, last)**
- **Learn about nurses.**
- **Learn about the newspaper.**
- **Learn about your nose.**
- **Learn about numbers.**

Art:

⇒ Make necklaces.
Cut the shape of an "N" out of sturdy paper. Glue nine noodles on the "N." Tie a string to the "N" and hang from neck. (Nice nine-noodle necklace)

⇒ Roll small amounts of dough and make a hole in center with toothpick. Let dry and paint with bright colors. String and tie around neck with yarn. *The day ahead, dip yarn in glue/water to make end stiff.

⇒ Purchase different types of noodles at grocery. Let children design with the noodles on study cardboard and then paint.

⇒ Purchase alphabet noodles and let children find the letters in their name and glue them on a card.

Tactile:

* Let children hammer small nails in a piece of wood. They may form an "N" with the nails.
* Write "Nn" on sturdy paper. Let children trace with glue and apply small noodles.
* Cut out an "N" shape from a newspaper and glue the newspaper "N" on a piece of construction paper.
* With marker draw an "N." Trace with glue. Sprinkle with nutmeg.

Baking:
◊   Cook noodles (different sizes and kinds)
◊   Make cookies and cut out in shapes of numbers.

Counting:
♥   Sort different kinds of noodles.
♥   Use small box to make a nest. Place in nest cards with different amounts of birds on each card. Let children pick a card with a number on it. Then they will reach in the nest to see if they can pick the card with birds which corresponds with the number card they have chosen.
♥   Name that Number: Hold up a number and let children say the number or hold up dots and let children say the number.

Games:
•   During recess, select an area to be the nest. Choose four children to be the two mothers and the two daddy birds. All the rest of the children will be the baby birds. When the baby birds leave the nest, the parent birds chase them. Once caught, baby birds cannot leave the nest until all are caught. Then choose four different parents.

Fieldtrips and Special Days:
➢   Visit a newspaper.
➢   Have a nurse visit the classroom.

Books:
Noisy Nancy Nora by Lou Ann Gaeddert
Noise in the Night by Anne Alexander
N is for Nursery School by Blossom Budney
Numbers by Jan Peinkowski
Night Noises by Mem Fox

Songs:

> **Tune to:** **"Skip to my Lou"**
> **Song:** **"What's Your Name?"**
> (Point to a child or let children pick each other to answer the questions after the song is sung)
>
> What's your name? Can you count to nine?
> What's your name? Can you count to nine?
> What's your name? Can you count to nine?
> (Pause) (Answer questions)
> That was very nice!
>
> (See Certificate for accomplishment above on p. 74)
>
> **Tune to:** **"Did You Ever See A Lassie?"**
> **Song:** **"Who is Your Neighbor?"**
> Who is your neighbor, your neighbor, your neighbor?
> Who is your neighbor standing (or sitting) right next to you?
>
> In front or behind you they're right next beside you
> Who is you neighbor? Please tell me right now.
>
> (Let each child tell who is standing or sitting in front of them and behind them.)
>
> **Tune to:** **"London Bridge is Falling Down"**
> **Song:** **"Nancy Needs a Napkin"**
>
> Nancy needs a napkin, a napkin, a napkin.
> Nancy needs a napkin to keep her new dress neat.

Fingerplay:

> I use my hammer and five nails.   (Show 5 fingers.)
> "That's too noisy," my neighbor yells!   (Raise voice.)
> I'll hammer them now before it's night!
> 1,2,3,4,5   (Pretend to hammer.)
> And to my neighbor I'll be polite!

Poem:

Naughty Ned

Naughty Ned, take your nap.
Take your nap right now!
I need to cook the noodles
and make the nest so neat.
So naughty Ned, what do you say
When I send you off to bed?
(All children say together)   NO!

Certificate for counting to nine and saying name

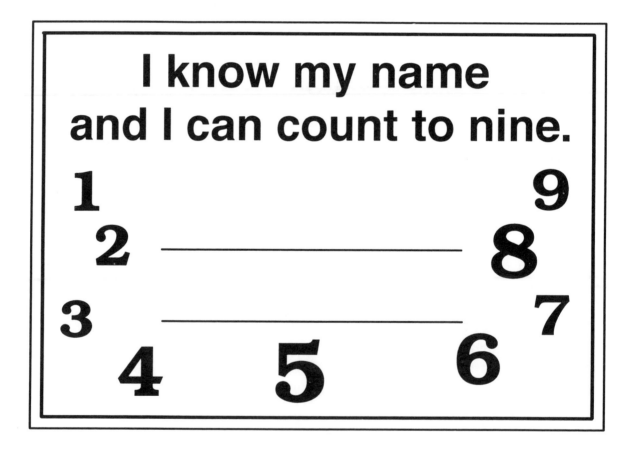

Always acknowledge children whose first or last name begins with letter that you are emphasizing.

NOTES:

Letter O Investigations:

- **Learn about oxen.**
- **Learn about an ostrich.**
- **Learn about an otter.**
- **Learn about opposites.**
- **Learn about an opera.**
- **Learn about oxygen.**
- **Learn about olives.**
- **Learn about ophthalmologist.**
- **Learn about an octagon.**

Art:

⇒ Draw or paint an octopus.

⇒ Paint or color green olives and put a red dot in center.

⇒ Put an octagon on an easel and let children trace around the edges.

Tactile:

* Draw an "O" and let children draw small green olives with red centers all around. Be sure to tell what olives are and let the children sample olives.

Baking:

◊ Make olive pizzas. Use hamburger buns and spread pizza sauce on the buns. Add slice olives, and top with cheese. Warm and serve. Great after school snack, too!

Counting:

♥ Paste different amounts of olives (made with green construction paper with red dots and some olives with black construction paper) on a sheet. Count the olives altogether or green and black olives separately. On the back, put the number for the green olives by a green olive and the number by a black olive. Also, put the total on back so children can check what they have counted.

♥ Count the legs of an octopus. What would happen if you grouped the legs in 2's, 3's, and 4's?

♥ Group other items in twos. Tell the children when one is always left over, this is called having an odd number.

Games:

- Look outside for Oscar: Use a small block or several blocks and tell the children that the block(s) represents an imaginary friend named Oscar. While the children have their backs turned, throw the blocks in different directions on the playground. Then call out, "Lookout for Oscar." Children then run and find the blocks. When a block is found, the child calls out "Oscar."

- Olive, Olive Who has the Olive? Sit on steps and let one or two children hold the olive made from a small piece of green paper or a green button and a painted red center. Other children pick which hand the olive is in. If correct, move to the next step; if incorrect, stay where you are.

Fieldtrips and Special Days:

➢ Visit an Ophthalmologist.
➢ Visit an observatory.
➢ Take a walk outside and observe.

Books:

Octopus by Evelyn S. Shaw
Oscar Otter by Nathaniel
Opposites by Denise Lewis-Patrick

Songs:

Tune to:　　　**"Twinkle, Twinkle Little Star"**
Song:　　　　**"Ollie Octopus"**
Ollie Octopus eats olives. This isn't odd; it's her occupation. After the opera in October, she eats olives all day long. /o/, /o/ Ollie had an operation. She'll have to give up her occupation.

Tune to: **"Baa, Baa, Black Sheep"**
Song: **"Opposites"**

Opposites are different things.
Here're a few that we will sing.
Loud and quiet, happy and sad,
Big and small, front and back.
Opposites are different things-
day and night and black and white.

Fingerplays:

Ostrich
An ostrich has two long legs
(Hold up 2 fingers.)

and can lay many large eggs.
(Touch together index fingers and thumb for large egg.)

She's the largest of all the birds,
(Hold hands up high like wings.)

And she can't fly. Isn't that absurd?
(Put hands on hips.)

Octopus
An octopus has 8 long arms.
(Hold up eight fingers.)

It lives in the sea, but do not be alarmed!
(Wave hands back and forth to indicate no harm.)

He squirts out ink, when he is the prey
(Clap hands when saying the word "squirts.")

and grows a new arm when it's torn away.
(Hold up an arm.)

Poem:

I Wish I was an Octopus
I wish I was an octopus.
I really wouldn't fuss,
For if I was an octopus,
I'd hug each one of us.

Poem:

Sore Throat
I went to the doctor just the other day.
I had a sore throat and I couldn't play.
The Doctor said, "Open very wide,"   (open mouth)
and all I could say was a great big _____!   (Make /o/ sound.)

Olive shapes   Octagon shape

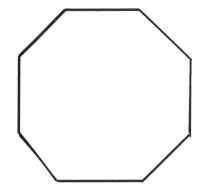

Always acknowledge children whose first or last name begins with letter that you are emphasizing.

NOTES:

Letter P Investigations:

- **Learn about penguins.**
- **Learn about poison prevention.**
- **Learn about plants.**
- **Learn about paper.**
- **Learn about pineapples.**
- **Learn about peanuts.**
- **Learn about parrots.**
- **Learn about pandas.**
- **Learn about the Pacific Ocean.**
- **Learn about pelicans.**

Art:

⇒ Potato Prints: Cut potatoes in half. Put them in paint and make prints.

⇒ Make a puppet with a sock.

⇒ Paint pink pigs.

⇒ Make a puzzle from a large picture. Glue piece of construction paper on back of child's picture or a picture from a magazine and let dry. Cut picture in large pieces to make puzzle.

⇒ Play with playdough. (Recipe on p. 137)

⇒ Paint pictures on paper plates.

Tactile:

∗ Draw "Pp" on cardboard. Let children use playdough to form the letters. Let dry and paint pink or purple.

∗ Put one dot of glue on a piece of paper. Put a pinch of pepper on the dot of glue. Let children draw "P's" on the paper.

∗ Glue popcorn to form "Pp."

∗ Put down sheets of waxed paper and let children finger paint with pudding.

Baking:

◊ Make pudding.

◊ Make popcorn.

◊ Make pizza.

Counting:

- ♥ Arrange items in pairs.
- ♥ Picking peas: Cut out green pea pods. On one side glue different amounts of peas. Draw a number from a container then pick a peapod to see if the number of peas match the number.
- ♥ Sort pencils or pens by color or length.
- ♥ Cut round pancakes out of cardboard. Let children count the amount in each stack.

Games:

- Pass the Potato, Please: Put music on and pass the potato until the music stops. When the music stops, the one with the potato says a word that starts with the /p/ sound.
- Parachute Play: Take a large parachute and let children hold on the edges. Let the children raise it high or wiggle it low. Let different children run under it when it is raised up high.

Fieldtrips and Special Days:

- ➤ Parents' Program Day. Children say poems, the Pledge of Allegiance, Kindergarten Prayer, Puppet show, and act out "The Three Little Pigs."
- ➤ "P" Picnic. Eat and drink things with the /p/ sound. Let children bring items to class. Send a note home requesting items such as:

  2 pears
  1 bag of pretzels
  1 bag of potato chips
  1 bag of popcorn
  1 jar of pickles
  1 can of pineapple
  paper plates
  punch
  Little Debbie's Pecan Pies

Assign two or three children the same items above and let each child have a sample of each thing. Let children acknowledge the item that he/she brought.

Books:
> Pablo Paints a Picture by Warren Miller
> Peggy and the Pony by Helen Moore Sewell
> Percy, Polly, and Pete by Clare Turlay Newberry
> Peter's Pocket by Judith Barrett

Songs:
> "Pease Porridge Hot" Nursery Rhyme
> "Peter Peter Pumpkin Eater" Nursery Rhyme

Sing "Peas In The Pot" from the "32 Natural Learning Songs from A-Z" cassette.

Tune to: **"Pop goes the Weasel"**
Song: **"Pig's Party"**
The Pigs are having a party.
They're popping lots of corn.
Please, pass your plate to put it on.
Pop, Pop, Pop, Pop, Pop!
(Children jump on the words, "Pop.")

Tune to: **"Polly Put the Kettle On"**
Song: **"Polly Plays a Piano"**
Polly plays a piano, a piano, a piano.
Polly plays a piano, ping, ping, pong!

Polly plays ping-pong, ping-pong, ping-pong.
Polly plays ping-pong, ping, ping, pong!

(Children may pretend to play a piano or ping-pong during song.)

Peter picked a perfect peach, perfect peach, perfect peach.
  (Children pretend to reach and pick a peach.)
Peter picked a perfect peach (pause)
  (Pretend to eat the peach during pause.)
and threw away the pit.
  (Pretend to throw away something.)
  (Ask children is they know what a pit is.)
In the second verse, "Penny" may be substituted

Fingerplays:

Pointy Fingers:

Two pointy fingers I can show	(Hold up both index fingers.)
Way up high or way down low.	(Hold index fingers high & low.)
With my right, I point to my toe.	(Right index toward toe.)
With my left, I show where to go.	(Point to left.)
Two pointy fingers I can show	(Hold up both index fingers.)
To show you things that I know!	(Point straight ahead, then to head.)

Pairs
Two things make a pair.
(Hold up two fingers.)

And on me, I'll show you where.
(Point to self.)

I have two ears, and I have two eyes.
(Point to ear and eyes.)

Both are important to make me wise!
I have two holes in my nose.
(Point to nose.)

That lets me smell a beautiful rose.
(Pretend to smell a rose.)

I have two hands that clap a beat.
(Clap hands to underlined words.)

I have two feet that are really neat!
(Jump when saying the word neat!)

Always acknowledge children whose first or last name begins with letter that you are emphasizing.

NOTES:

Letter Q Investigations:

- **Learn about quills.**
- **Learn about quails.**
- **Learn about quarts.**
- **Learn about earthquakes.**
- **Learn about quartz.**
- **Learn about quarters.**

Art:

⇒ Make crowns for Queens in class.
(Crown pattern p. 58)

⇒ Design quilts. (Glue squares of material on paper to design own quilt. Combine all the quilt designs for a quilt bulletin board. Use strips between squares.)

⇒ Take quarters and place under a piece of paper. Make etchings with the quarters.

Tactile:

* Quilt "Q" … Teacher draw a "Q" on piece of paper with a marker. Children may either color with different colors or may glue small squares of material on the "Q."

* Make a question mark out of playdough on sturdy paper. Let dry and paint. Ask children to make up a question!

Baking:

◊ Make question marks out of biscuit dough and bake.
◊ Make Quaker brand oatmeal

Counting:

- ♥ From quarter etchings (use different colors), cut out circles of quarters and glue to sturdy circles the same size. Sort different colors of quarters. Then count each stack of quarters.
- ♥ If everyone in the room was either a king or a queen, how many queens would you have and how many kings?

Games:

- Give children books and magazines. Divide children in groups and see who can find question marks. When a question mark is found in a group, a mark can be placed by that group, and each group's score may be tallied at the end of the time period.
- Have a duck race. Let children squat and walk like a duck a short distance and return. They must touch the next one in line and say "quack" to let the next person go.
- Play the Quiet Game.

Fieldtrips and Special Days:

- ➢ Have a Question Day. Let children ask questions. Teacher may write the questions on a large sheet emphasizing the question mark at the end. Talk about the question with class or teacher answering the question.
- ➢ Visit the library to find answers to some questions. Emphasize the importance of being very quiet in the library.

Books:

Quack? by Mischa Richter
Quiet! There's a Canary in the Library by Don Freeman
The Very Quiet Cricket by Eric Carle

Songs:

    Tune to: **"Mary Had a Little Lamb"**
    Song: **"Letter "Q"**

Where, oh where, is the letter "Q?"   Letter "Q?" Letter "Q?"
Where, oh where, is the letter "Q?"
Go quickly and ask the Queen!

I have found the letter "Q", Letter "Q", Letter "Q."
I have found the letter "Q."
I found it under the quilt!

    Tune to: **"The Farmer in the Dell"**
    Song: **"Quiet Time"**

We must be very quiet.
We must be very quiet.
We put up our things and stand in line.
We must be very quiet!

(In the second verse, substitute "quick.")
(Sing softly when getting ready to leave the room. Sing three or four times and each time sing a little quieter. Hopefully, everyone will be whispering the song and standing in line ready to go after about 3 or 4 verses.)

Fingerplay:
Five Little Ducks and Five Little Quail

Five little ducks went out to play
(Wiggle five fingers on right hand.)

And met five quail that came their way.
(Wiggle five fingers on left hand.)

The five little quail went to get a snack,
(Take left hand to behind back.)

And the five little ducks went "quack, quack, quack!"
(Put right hand to mouth like a duck's bill and move fingers as imitating duck quacking.)

Five Queens

There were 5 queens on a quest   (Hold up five fingers.)
To see who was the very best!   (Wiggle all five.)
The first queen went to take a test.   (Touch thumb.)
The second queen said, "I'll go out west."   (Touch index.)
The third queen climbed Mount Everest.   (Touch middle.)
The fourth queen made a beautiful vest.   (Touch ring.)
The fifth queen said, "I'll just take a rest." (Touch little finger.)

Always acknowledge children whose first or last name begins with letter that you are emphasizing.

NOTES:

Letter R Investigations:

- **Learn about rainbows.**
- **Learn about raisins.**
- **Learn about rabbits.**
- **Learn about Robin Red Breast.**
- **Learn about rectangles.**
- **Learn about raccoons.**
- **Learn about rain.**

Art:

⇒ Make pictures using different colors of ribbon. Let the children be creative in their creations.

⇒ Color or paint rainbow pictures.

⇒ Make red recipe books. Use recipes that have been used in class or will be used later. Let children decorate pages by drawing pictures of what the recipe make.

⇒ Collects some rocks. The rocks may be sorted by size or color. Let children glue smaller rocks to cardboard. Let children draw or paint a picture with the rocks.

⇒ Let children paint a rock and design a pet rock.

Tactile:

* Red Rice "R's." Teacher can write "R" on sturdy paper with a marker. Let children apply glue and sprinkle red rice on the glue. Dye the rice before by using small amount of rubbing alcohol and red food coloring. Dry rice on a paper towel.

Baking:

◊ Make round raisin cookies.

◊ Make Rice Crispy treats.

◊ Cook instant rice.

Counting:

- ♥ Count rocks.
- ♥ Cut out rectangles of different sizes. (Rectangles may be sorted or counted.)
- ♥ Let children find things that are round in the room and count them.
- ♥ Count how many right-handed children there are in the classroom. Graph the results.
- ♥ Let everyone who has red on stand up and count the children.

Games:

- Red Rover
- Ring Around the Roses
- Remembering Game: On a tray, put several objects. Let the children at a table close their eyes. Remove one or more objects from the tray. Let the children try to remember what was on the tray and what was removed.

Fieldtrips and Special Days:

- ➤ Wear Red Day… Encourage children to wear at least one thing red one day. If a child forgets, safety pen a red ribbon to their clothing.
- ➤ Rhyming Day…Encourage children throughout the day to tell words that rhyme.

Books:

Ricky the Raccoon by Alain Gree, Louis Camp
Rain, Rain, Rivers by Uri Shulevitz
Ring O' Roses Mother Goose
Round Things Everywhere by Seymour Reit
Red is Best by Kathy Stinson

Songs:

Tune to: "Row, Row, Row Your Boat"
Song: "Row Your Raft"
Row, row, row, your raft
Racing down the river.
Raining, raining, raining,
Racing in the rain!

Tune to: "Old MacDonald"
Song: "Rhyming Song"

Tell me a word that rhymes with **AT**--
at, fat, cat.
(repeat)

With an at, at, here and an at, at, there.
Here an at, there an at, everywhere at, at

Tell me a word that rhymes with **AT**--
AT, AT, _____

2nd verse
Tell me a word that rhymes with **IG**--
ig, wig, big.

(Substitute IG with rest of verse.)

3rd verse
Tell me a word that rhymes with **OT**--
ot, dot, lot

(Substitute OT with rest of verse.)

Fingerplay:
Way up high, little robin flying just so.
(Put hands up high.)

Quick down low for a worm he must go.
(Put hands down low.)

With a wing on the left and a wing on the right,
(Extend arms one at a time, left first, then right.)

Fly to your nest for soon it will be night.
(Flap arms as if flying.)

Sing "Riding with Ricky" from the "More Natural Learning Songs from A-Z" cassette or "Rhyme Song" from the "32 Natural Learning Songs from A-Z" cassette.

Poem:

    I remember Every Rule
    I remember every rule
    whether I'm home or here at school.
    Rules are good; they really rate.
    They help me to become someone great!

GOLDEN RULE

Do unto others as you would have them do unto you.

Always acknowledge children whose first or last name begins with letter that you are emphasizing.

NOTES:

Letter S Investigations:

- **Learn about spiders.**
- **Learn about scorpions.**
- **Learn about The Statue of Liberty.**
- **Learn about our Solar System.**
- **Learn about seasons.**
- **Learn about seeds.**
- **Learn about the Sun.**
- **Learn about snakes.**
- **Learn about salmon.**

Art:

⇒ Paint spiders.

⇒ Let children pick a season and paint a picture during that season.

⇒ Let whole class color a mural showing each season: fall, winter, spring, summer.

⇒ Color heavy with a yellow crayon on a piece of paper. Then color with a black crayon on top of the yellow. Scratch out a little of the black crayon to let the yellow sun show through.

⇒ Make a beach picture and let children sprinkle sand on their picture. Encourage children to have a sun in their pictures. Ask children what is important to put on our skin before going out into the sunshine. (sun screen)

⇒ Paint or draw smiley faces.

⇒ Make puppets using socks. (A snake puppet for letter "S" would be sensational!)

Tactile:

* Teacher writes Letter "Ss" with marker on sturdy pieces of paper. Children apply glue and sprinkle sand or seeds on glue.

Baking:

◊ Read <u>Stone Soup</u> by Marcia Brown and follow the recipe in the book.

◊ Read <u>Chicken Soup with Rice</u> by Maurice Sendak and make chicken soup.

◊ Make this simple soup. Mix together:
   1 large can of V-8 juice
   water (about ½ of the V-8 can)
   1 can of cream of corn
   1 summer sausage cut into small pieces
   1 can of Veg-All
   Cook for about 45 minutes to one hour
   Serves 10-12 very small servings.

Counting:

♥ Count the legs of a spider.

♥ Sort socks and count them.

♥ Emphasize the numbers six and seven.

♥ Count stories in a building.

♥ Count everyone who has shoes with *strings.*

♥ Count everyone who is wearing *sandals.*

♥ Sort and count spoons.

Games:

• Simon Says

• I Spy

• Smelling Game: Put things that smell in an empty 35 mm film container. Puncture the top with several holes. Put a cotton ball in each one and add different things, such as perfume, peppermint, lemon flavoring, vanilla flavoring, cherry juice, etc. Let children try to identify the smells.

Fieldtrips and Special Days:

➤ Bring a microscope to class for children to view spiders.

➤ Visit a super market. (A lot of /s/ sounds will be in there.)

Books:

Sammy the Seal by Sydney Hoff
School for Sillies by Jay Williams
The Seasame Street Song Book Illus. By Loretta Trezzo
Six Silver Spoons by Janette Sebring Lowrey
(*See baking section for more books.*)

Songs:

Tune to:	**"Three Blind Mice"**
Song:	**"Six Silly Snakes"**

Six silly snakes, six silly snakes
Singing a song, Singing a song,
They slither and slide by the sandy sea.
They smile when they see the letter "S"--
/s/, /s/, /s/, /s/, /s/, /s/ .

Tune to:	**"On Top of Old Smokey"**
Song:	**"Singing in my Saddle"**

I sit on my saddle on my horse named Sal.
I sing this sweet song to Susie my gal. (May substitue "Sammy my pal.")

I sing this song softly.   (Sing softly.)
I sing it slowly.   (Sing slowly.)

I'll sing it six times.
In the summertime.

Tune to:	**"The Farmer in the Dell"**
Song:	**"Action Song"**

I'm standing very straight,   (Stand up.)
and now I sitting down.   (Sit.)
I snap my fingers twice,   (Snap twice.)
and then I give a smile.   (Smile.)

Tune to: "Are You Sleeping"
Song: "Sleeping Song"
Are you sleeping, are you sleeping,
Silly Sue, Silly Sue?   (or Silly Sam)
The sun is smiling on you.
There's something you must do ---
Go to school, go to school.

Fingerplay:

Six silly spiders standing in a row.	(Hold up six fingers.)
They just do not know where to go,	(Wiggle 6 fingers.)
But when someone comes to spray,	(Pretend to spray; use /s/ sound.)
They will be off on their way.	(Wiggle fingers away.)

Fingerplay:

In the sea are seven seals.	(Hold up 7 fingers.)
Swimming and splashing are some of their skills.	(Pretend to swim.)
Soon the seals are surprised.	(Throw hand up as surprised.)
By a fish that's twice their size.	

(As voice gets louder, put arms out wide to show big.)

Swim, little seals, as swiftly as you can,	(Pretend to swim fast.)
Or there may be only six in your clan.	(Hold up six fingers.)

Poem:

I'm going swimming in the sea.	(Pretend to swim.)
I have an intertube just for me!	(Point to self.)
I hear a sound. What could it be? /sssssssss/	(Hold hand to ear.)
A hole in my tube, would you agree?	

Always acknowledge children whose first or last name begins with letter that you are emphasizing.

NOTES:

Letter T Investigations:

- **Learn about trains.**
- **Learn about turtles.**
- **Learn about teeth.**
- **Learn about turkeys.**
- **Learn about tigers.**
- **Learn about the telephone.**
- **Learn about the television.**

Art:

⇒ Make tabourines with paper plates. Put pebbles in the middle and staple around the edges. Add streamers and decorate plates.

⇒ Draw trees.

⇒ Trace toes.

⇒ Make tennis ball puppets. Teacher must make the basic puppet. Draw mouth on tennis ball with red marker. With an ice pick put hole in center of red mouth. Use a pointed steak knife to place in the ice pick hole and finish cutting the mouth. Let children decorate and make eyes with markers. Children can also glue yarn for hair. *Great for children to use to strengthen muscles in hand and fingers.*

Tactile:

* Teacher writes "T" on sturdy paper or cardboard. Children apply glue and may put toothpicks to form "T."

* Children may sprinkle tea from teabag on the glue.

* Practice tying shoelaces.

Baking:

◊ Toast: Let children paint "T" on the toast with food color; then add butter. Toast may be cut into triangles.

◊ Cook tater tots.

◊ Make tea for the class to drink.

Counting:
- ♥ Emphasize the numbers two and ten.
- ♥ Count toes.
- ♥ Count by tens.
- ♥ Count teeth that the children have lost.
- ♥ Make toadstools and put numbers on the toadstools. Let children place the corresponding amount of toads on the toadstools.
- ♥ Look at animal tails. See how they are alike or different from other tails.
- ♥ Learn about triangles.
- ♥ Cut out the ten toads in the art section. (See p. 156) Glue each one on a square piece of construction paper. Let the children take turns counting them.

Games:
- • Play Tag.
- • Have a treasure hunt for the letter "T" or /t/ sound items in the room.
- • Play Tic-Tac-Toe.
- • Use a block or something to symbolize a turkey. All of the children must close their eyes while one child hides the turkey. Then he/she must count to ten. The rest of the class may walk around the room and find the turkey. The one who finds the turkey may hide it next.

Fieldtrips and Special Days:
- ➤ Terrific Tuesday: Have a tasting tea.
- ➤ Visit a train station.
- ➤ Visit a television station.

Books:
The Tale of Mrs. Tittlemouse by Beatrix Potter
Ten Apples Up on Top! by Theodor Suess Geisel
Timothy Turtle by Alice V. Davis
Teddy Bear's Book of 1,2,3 by Betty Ren Wright

Songs:

Tune to: **"Jimmy Crack Corn"**
Song: **"Too Tired"**

I'm too tired to touch my toes.   (Pretend to touch toes.)
I'm too tired to touch my toes.   (Pretend to touch toes.)
I'm too tired to touch my toes.   (Pretend to touch toes.)
I'll just touch my top!   (Touch top of head.)

Tune to: **"For He's a Jolly Good Fellow"**
Song: **"Ten Toads"**

Ten toads in the teepee.   (Hold up 10 fingers for toads and then touch
Ten toads in the teepee.   fingertips together to form teepee.)
Ten toads in the teepee.   (Form a "T" by placing tip of fingers under
Together they're a team!   middle of the other arm.)

Tune to: **"Baa, Baa, Black Sheep"**
Song: **"Tick Tock"**

Tick tock, two o'clock tiptoe in the town.
Tommy told the teacher Tammy's on TV.
Tomorrow is Tuesday; my toes are tired.
Isn't it time to trick or treat?

Tick tock, two o'clock tiptoe in the town.
"T" is terrific-- /t/, /t/, /t/.

Fingerplay:

Two tiny toads jumping around.
(Hold up 2 fingers and turn around.)

Two turtles crawling on the ground.
(Hold up 2 fingers and bend down low.)

They all tiptoed without making a sound.
(Hold up 4 fingers and tiptoe.)

And they turned their heads round and round.
(Turn heads round and round.)

---

10 toes way down low,   (Point to toes.)
Arms out just like so!   (Put both arms straight out.)
Head high in the shade,   (Put head up.)
Letter T, I have made!

Poem:

I have two friends that look just alike.
(Hold up both index fingers.)

One's name is Ike, and the other's name is Mike.
(Show one index for Ike and the other for Mike.)

When they trick the teacher, they just grin.
(Smile)

They are known as the troublesome twins.
(Shake finger.)

Always acknowledge children whose first or last name begins with letter that you are emphasizing.

NOTES:

Letter U Investigations:

- **Learn about understanding others' feelings.**
- **Learn about times to use an umbrella.**
- **Learn about things that are under other things.**
- **Learn about things that are up.**

Art:

⇒ Create a picture of yourself with an umbrella on a day that you would need one. Let the children tell about their picture.

⇒ Read and discuss the story about "The Ugly Duckling." Talk about how the ugly duckling felt at first and then at the end. Let the children draw a mural of the story.

⇒ Cut a piece of blue or green cellophane. Staple it to the top of a piece of white construction paper. Let children create a picture on the white paper of things that would be under the water. (Optional: Talk about undertows in the water.)

Tactile:

* On a piece of paper, let children trace a "U" that you have already drawn on the paper. Then tell the children to draw an umbrella so that the "U" will be under the umbrella.

Counting:

♥ On several different boards, glue different amounts of umbrellas. Let the children count the umbrellas and say the appropriate number. Have the number on the back for the children to see the number after they say it.

♥ Count the large fish in the underwater picture in art.

Games:

- Say different words. When the children hear a word that begins with /u/, they are to stand "UP." If the word does not, they remain seated.
- Understanding feelings: Talk about different situations that might happen in the room. Let children discuss how they might feel.

  Examples: New person comes into the room.

  Sally is sitting by herself on the playground.

  Billy cried when someone laughed at his picture.

  Jane has to have a wheelchair to get around.

Fieldtrips and Special Days:

- ➢ Invite an uncle to come and read a story to the class.
- ➢ Act out the story of "The Ugly Duckling."
- ➢ Make Unusual faces in the classroom or outside while Under the Umbrella.

Books:

The Ugly Duckling by Hans Christian Andersen

Umbrella by Jun Iwamatsu

Under the Window by Kate Greenaway

Upside Down by David Johnson Leisk

Umbrella by Taro Yashima

Songs:

Tune to: **"London Bridge"**

Song: **The Letter "U"**

The letter "U" is going up, going up, going up.

The letter "U" is going up. Do you Understand?

(Teacher or students may hold "U's" in hand and move their hand up or stand up in the song.)

Fingerplay:

> Under my umbrella, I am dry.
> (Cup hand above index finger.)
>
> When it's raining, my oh my.
> (Fingers wiggle like rain coming down.)
>
> I wait until the raindrops stop.
> (Clap hands together on the word "stop.")
>
> Now no umbrella on my top!
> (Just hold up index finger.)

Fingerplay:

> I point one finger up.   (Point index finger up.)
> I point one finger down.   (Point other index finger down.)
> I point one finger under my chin.   (Hold finger sideways under nose.)
> And then I make a great big grin!   (Smile.)

Poem:

> My dog and I like to walk in the rain.
> I carry an umbrella when we walk down the lane.
> When I clean my shoes on the outside rug,
> My mother gives me a great big hug.
> Buttercup runs past me; he's just a pup.
> And mother says, "You'll have to clean that up!"

Always acknowledge children whose first or last name begins with letter that you are emphasizing.

NOTES:

Letter V Investigations:

- **Learn about volcanoes.**
- **Learn about vegetables.**
- **Learn about violins.**
- **Learn about your voice.**
- **Learn about vowels.**
- **Learn about voting.**

Art:

⇒ Paint a picture of violets in a vase.

⇒ Make a volcano. Use a 35 mm tube used to hold film. Smooth home-made flour dough or dough that air dries. Place dough around the sides of the tube to form the shape of a volcano. Paint dough brown and let sit overnight to dry in an aluminum pie plate. (Be sure to put names on the pie plates for the next day.) Next day, let the volcanoes erupt. Put one teaspoon of baking soda in all of the tubes. Add red food coloring to small amount of vinegar. (You will need about 1 tablespoon for each volcano.) Add about 1 tablespoon of red vinegar to soda mixture in tube. Mixture will bubble out like a volcano erupting. Start collecting pie pans early in the year so each child may erupt his/her volcano at school and at home without making a mess!

⇒ Paint using different vegetable as stamps.

Tactile:

* On a piece of paper, let children trace a "V" that you have already written on the paper. Then let the children cut out several Valentine hearts and glue them around the "V." With one Valentine heart, attach a small amount of Velcro to the paper and to the heart for an added /v/ sound.

* Mix a small amount of vanilla flavoring in light purple or Violet color. Let children paint a violet colored "V" and then see if they smell the vanilla flavoring.

* Cut small strips of velvet or velvet-like fabric. Let children make velvet "V."

* Let the children make visors. (See art section p. 155)

Baking:

◊ Let children try samples of vegetables with dip.

◊ Make vegetable soup (Great for family, too!)

        1 large can V-Eight juice

        Use about 1/2 of can to add water

        Add 1 can of creamed corn

        Add 1 can mixed vegetables

        Simmer for at least 45 minutes

        *Optional... May add cooked chicken/beef

        *Optional... May add summer sausage

◊ Make vanilla milk shakes.

◊ Make vanilla pudding or ice cream.

Counting:

♥ Count Valentines. Draw a number from a small stack of cards. Let children match the number with that amount of Valentine hearts.

♥ Count vans that pass by the school. (Mini vans count) If you divided the children into groups which represent colors, then the response can be graphed. For example, divide children in five groups: Blue, Red, White, Black, Green. When a van passes which is close to their color, one person in the group will receive a token of some kind. At the end of 10 minutes, graph the response. Maybe a group might be needed to represent an unknown color when it passes. Do this more than once and compare graphs.

♥ Vote on something in the room. Example: coloring with markers or coloring with crayons, singing a song or saying a fingerplay, playing with blocks or playing with puzzles. Explain that you will say two things; to vote each child may raise his/her hand once or go to a specific area to state their decision. Then count to see how the voting went.

Games:
- Play volley ball with a soft ball and low net.
- Vanishing "V": Take the letter "V" and hide it in the room. Select one person or several to close their eyes while you hide the "V." Give the child/children clues by raising the volume of your voice when one is getting near the "V" or softly instruct any children who are going away from the "V."

Fieldtrips and Special Days:
➢ Invite a veterinarian to the classroom.
➢ Invite someone who plays a violin to come to the classroom.
➢ Visit a vegetable garden.

Books:
The Very First Day by Ann Weil
The Very Hungry Caterpillar by Eric Carle
The Village Tree by Jun Iwamatsu

Songs:
Tune to: **"The Farmer in the Dell"**
Song: **"The Letter "V"**

The volume of my voice goes up or down of course!
It's LOUD or *soft* or very nice,
The volume of my voice.

I vacuum through the house.
I vacuum through the house.
The dirt has vanished from the floor
when I vacuum through the house.

Volume control: Cut out volume control and brad to a paper plate. Add numbers around control for children to increase or decrease volume. Place a volume control on the wall in the classroom. Instruct the children that they must whisper when the control is pointing toward 1,2, or 3. They may talk normally with the control on 4, 5, or 6. When the control is on 7, 8, or 9, the class may be loud.   Tell the class that the volume control is never set on 10; ten is only for emergencies, 0 is for quiet.

Tune to: **"Where Oh Where Has My Little Dog Gone?"**
Song: **"Vanishing "V"**

Where, oh where is my vanishing "V?"
Oh where, oh where can it be?
Will it visit the vet or hide in a vase?
Where, oh where can it be?

(Have fun with Nursery Rhyme songs. Sing using different voices: high, low   loud, soft   fast, slow.)

Poem or Rap:
I have on my vest and my visor too!
(Touch chest and hold hand over eyes.)

They are new and the color is blue!
(Clap on "new" and on "blue.")

I'm riding in my van and taking in the view.
(Pretend to be driving.)

Maybe next time you can come, too!
(Still pretend to be driving.)

(Tell the class that to veer means to turn. Tell the class to veer to the left and veer to the right.)

Rebus:

Key words:

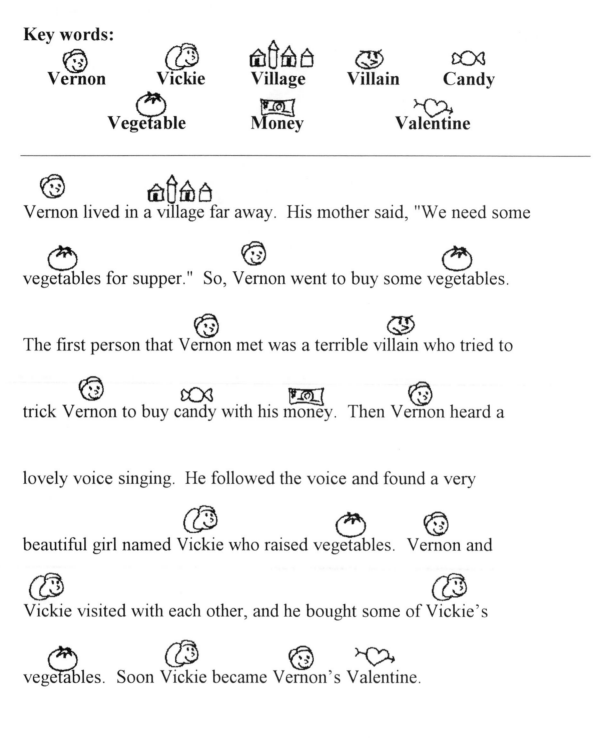

Vernon lived in a village far away. His mother said, "We need some

vegetables for supper." So, Vernon went to buy some vegetables.

The first person that Vernon met was a terrible villain who tried to

trick Vernon to buy candy with his money. Then Vernon heard a

lovely voice singing. He followed the voice and found a very

beautiful girl named Vickie who raised vegetables. Vernon and

Vickie visited with each other, and he bought some of Vickie's

vegetables. Soon Vickie became Vernon's Valentine.

Always acknowledge children whose first or last name begins with letter that you are emphasizing.

NOTES:

Letter W Investigations:

- **Learn about water.**
- **Learn about our national capital, Washington, D.C.**
- **Learn about worms.**
- **Learn about watermelons.**
- **Learn about a walrus.**
- **Learn about wasps.**
- **Learn about winter.**
- **Learn about wolves.**

Art:

⇒ Make watermelon pictures. Glue on dried watermelon seeds or paint black dots as seeds.

⇒ Paint or draw with markers on scrap pieces of wood.

⇒ Draw a large window on a large box and cut out. Let children use their imagination to what they see out of the window. Each child may take a turn and stand in the box at the window.

⇒ Let children draw a picture with different types of weather. Let the children tell about their pictures.

⇒ Let children paint wiggle worms.

⇒ Let children design a picture using wallpaper.

⇒ Let the children draw a picture of themselves in water getting wet.

⇒ Let the children make wallets. (See art section p. 157)

Tactile:

* Cut out wallpaper strips to form a "W."

* Roll a long worm out of playdough and form a "W"

* Make wax paper "W." Let children design a "W" with wallpaper and glue the "W" to the wax paper.

* Let children trace a "W" with glue. Children then apply small pieces of weeds for a "Weedy W."

Baking:

◊ Make watermelon flavored gelatin.

◊ Roll cookie dough into long worms and bake.

◊ Make waffles with a waffle iron or buy them at grocery and bake.

Counting:

♥ Have different pictures with different amounts of watermelon seeds on them. Let the children count the seeds. Say the number and then look on back to see the number.

♥ Count the windows in you room and in other rooms.

♥ Count the days in a week.

♥ Weigh each child for his/her weight.

♥ Count walnuts. Place walnuts in large bowl. Put a number on a smaller bowl. Let the children put the appropriate number of walnuts in each bowl.

♥ Take 5 to 10 sheets of wallpaper. Cut them into squares and mix up. Let the children sort the wallpaper and match all the like pieces together.

♥ Make sheets with different amounts of worms. You may have one color of worms per sheet or you may have different colors. Make the worms large enough for the children to see. For each sheet, ask how many worms and/or what color worms are. Optional: If you have two green worms and two yellow ones on a sheet, you may ask for the total amount of worms on the sheet.

Games:

- I Went on a Walk and Watched the _____. Each child says the sentence and fills in the blank with his/her imagination. The game may be filled in alphabetical. For example: Teacher starts: I went on a walk and watched the alligators; (First student:) I went on a walk and watched the birds. Next student will say a word with the /k/ sound which begins with the letter "C."

- Teacher will give different instructions to children who are wearing different colors and then children sit down. Example: All children wearing red stand up; then sit down. All children wearing blue, hop on one foot and then sit down. All children wearing green, walk to the door and touch it and then sit down. All children wearing a dress, walk around the table and then sit down.

Fieldtrips and Special Days:

- ➤ Have a Wonderful Wednesday and make a welcome mat for the classroom.
- ➤ Take a pretend walk in the woods and tell what you see.
- ➤ Read about and show pictures of Washington, D. C. Talk about what you might see there.
- ➤ Have a friend or yourself to be "Wonder Woman" named Wendy. Wear a wig and wear warm ups with a "W" on the front and back. Cape is optional. Wonder Woman is very smart but instruct the children that we will use a different word that begins with /w/ this week for smart. (wise) The children can show and tell Wonder Woman all the /w/ sounds that they have talked about this week!
- ➤ Take an imaginary trip around the world.

Books:

Wacky Wednesday by Theordor Seuss Geusel

Wait for William by Marjorie Flack

The Wump World by Bill Peet

Where the Wild Things Are by Maurice Sendak

Songs:

> **Tune to:**   **"Mary Had a Little Lamb"**
> **Song:**   **"Walk Around the World"**

I woke up on a Wednesday morn, Wednesday morn, Wednesday morn.
I woke up on a Wednesday morn and walked around the world.

If you wade in the water, you might get wet, might get wet, might get wet. If you wade in the water, you might get wet, woo woo woo woo woo.

I made a wish at the wishing well, wishing well, wishing well. I made a wish at the wishing well. I wonder if it will come true.

> **Tune to:**   **"London Bridge is Falling Down"**
> **Song:**   **"Washing"**

I wash myself with water, water, water.
I wash myself with water, and I wash with soap!

Sing "Willie the Worm" from the "More Natural Learning Songs from A-Z" cassette.

Fingerplays:

A wonderful world, I live in
(Make a circle.)

I watch the worms, and I count to 10.
(Hold up 10 fingers.)

I wash my window way up high
(Pretend to wash window up high.)

And walk in the woods and wave good-bye!
(Walk in place and wave good-bye.)

Fingerplay:

5 wasps were on the wall.
(Show 5 fingers.)

How could they hurt me, they are so small!
(Put hands on waist.)

I'll spray some water, so they will fall.
(Pretend to spray water with hose.)

Uh oh! I'd better run! They're after me, five wasps in all!
(Wiggle 5 fingers.)

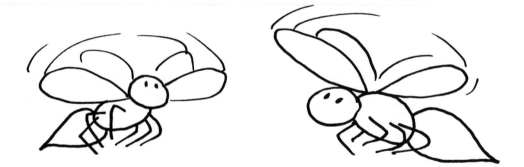

Always acknowledge children whose first or last name begins with letter that you are emphasizing.

NOTES:

Letter X Investigations:

- Emphasize <u>x</u> sounding /ks/ at the end of the word. Example: fox, box, fix, ax, tax, fax, tux, six…
- Let each child bring a large box to school to create his/her own means of transportation. Cut out part of the top of the box for the child to be able to put body through and stand through box. Cut about a six inch line on both sides of the box where the child may grasp and hold the box up. Let the children paint the boxes outside in a grassy area. Have available construction paper for children to make headlights, license plates, controls, etc. My class made everything from a helicopter, 4 wheel-drive truck, to a pink Cadilac. Then we all sang the song "Take me Riding in your Bumpity Bus," and we substituted each vehicle, and that person would drive his/her vehicle during the song.
- Children love to play in boxes. Bring a large box to the classroom and let the children decorate it. Some ideas are: puppet stage, a post office, a service station, the White House, etc. Let the children use their imagination.

Art:

⇒ Color a picture on wax paper.
⇒ Divide the children into groups with 6 children in each group. Before hand, find boxes and wrap them in newsprint. Mark each side of the box with numbers 1-6(and dots) with a marker. Assign each child a number and let the children decorate their side in each group. Let the children have show and tell with their box side. Taking turns is important here also! While children 1-4 will have their sides showing and #5 will have his/hers on top, #6 will have to wait. Let him/her be planning and creating things to put on his/her side.

Tactile:

* Let children finger-paint X's on paper or small box.
* Let children trace over an X with a marker. **Danger** **Be Careful** With teacher holding child's hand, let child drip a couple of drops of wax from a birthday candle on the X. ***(Teacher may do this herself/himself away from children.)
* Take pretzel sticks and form X's then eat!

Baking:
◊   Form X's with cookie dough and bake.

Counting:
♥   Let children count the sides of several boxes. How many sides does every box have?

♥   In one big box, have several small boxes. Wrap the smaller boxes with different gift-wrap. When the children are not looking, take one or two boxes out. Let the children try to guess which box/boxes were taken out. The children can also take turns counting the boxes.

♥   Draw different amounts of large X's on poster paper. Let the children count them and then look on the back of the poster paper to see if they said the correct number.

♥   On some board, put X's and Y's. Let the children point only to X's on the board. Put the correct amount on the back.

Games:
•   Play Tic-tac-toe then count the number of X's.

•   Fox in the Box: Choose three or four persons to be "It." Let the other children be foxes. Indicate a "place" on the playground to be the box. When a person who is "It" catches a fox, they must yell "Fox in the Box." The fox must go to the box area, and stay until all foxes are caught. Then select other persons to be "It."

Fieldtrips and Special Days:
➢   Play with the vehicle boxes on the playground. Video tape the children and then watch it.

➢   Invite someone who plays the sax to visit the classroom.

Books:

The Fox and the Fire by Miska Miles
Six Foolish Fishermen by Benjonie Elkin
Six in a Mix by Jack E. Richardson, Jr.
Rex by Marjorie Weinman Sharmat
Inside outside Upside Down by Stan and Jan Berenstain
Fox in Socks by Dr. Seuss
Fox in a Fix by Lois Dean

Songs:

Tune to: **"The Farmer in the Dell"**
Song: **"X" Song"**

I make a little "X."	(Cross two fingers.)
I make a bigger "X."	(Cross arms.)
I make larger "X."	(Spread arms and legs out to form "X.")
And then I start again.	(Bring arms and legs back to side.)

Tune to: **"Frog Went A Courtin'"**
Song: **"Ending Sounds of "X"**

Can you hear the ending sounds of "X?"---/ks/
Can you hear the ending sounds of "X?"---/ks/
"Box" and "fox" and "chickenpox"
"ax" and "max", "wax" and "tax",
Can you hear the ending sounds of "X?"---/ks/
(Repeat)

Fingerplay:

I saw a little fox	(Hold up two fingers walking in air.)
climb into a box.	(Put fingers in opening of other hand.)
I saw a large ox	(Hold hand as a fist.)
sit on a mailbox.	(Place fist on other hand.)

Always acknowledge children whose first or last name begins with letter that you are emphasizing.

NOTES:

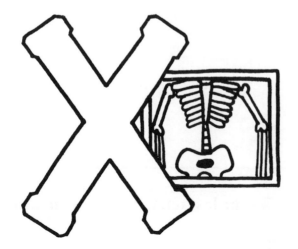

Letter Y Investigations:

- **Learn about yachts.**
- **Learn about yaks.**
- **Learn about yams.**
- **Learn about yellow.**
- **Learn about yodeling.**
- **Learn about yourself.**

Art:

⇒ Use yellow yarn to make pictures.
⇒ Finger-paint with yellow pudding. (lemon or banana flavor)
⇒ Draw a picture of yourself.

Tactile:

* Glue yellow yarn to form a "Y."
* Paint yellow "Y's."

Baking:

◊ Bake and slice yams for children to taste.
◊ Make bread with yeast.
◊ Boil eggs and cut them in two halves. Let children see the yolk.

Counting:

♥ Show different types of potatoes and let children tell how they are different and how they are alike.
♥ Count yo-yo's... Draw yo-yo's on pieces of manila paper. Let children count the yo-yo's and say the number. Have the correct number on the back.
♥ Ask how many years old each child is and graph the results.

Games:

- Yakety Yak Don't talk Back.
  Children sit in a circle and must not talk. One child chooses two children to come to the center of the circle. As he/she chooses, he/she says, "Yakety Yak Don't Talk Back." The children will stand in the center. The one child may pass out cards with animal pictures to the two children. These children must act like these animals. The other children guess what they are acting out. If someone guess correctly, the child who is acting must say, "Yakety Yak!"

Fieldtrips and Special Days:

➤ Wear Something Yellow Day.

➤ Visit a yogurt Shop.

➤ Yo-yo Day. Children bring yo-yo's (Teacher may have some yo-yo's in the classroom that the children may share.)

Books:

Yakety Yak-Yak-Yak by Richard Hefter

Yellow Yellow by Frank Asch

You and the World Around You Millicent Ellis Selsam

Yummers! by James Marshall

The Yellow Boat by Margaret Hillert

Songs:

Tune to: **"Mary Had a Little Lamb"**

Song: **"Yell for Yellow"**

You can yell for yellow, yellow, yellow.
You can yell for yellow, and you can yodel too!

Tune to: **"The Farmer in the Dell"**

Song: **"Yak is in the Yard"**

The yak is in the yard. The yak is in the yard.
Yes, yes you must agree. The yak is in the yard.

Fingerplay:

Five yaks yawned a lot--	(Hold up 5 fingers and yawn.)
Time for bed believe it or not	(Lay hands aside of face as asleep.)
For your mother you must obey.	(Shake pointy finger.)
And when you get up,	(Jump up and say "yea.")
just yell yea!	

Always acknowledge children whose first or last name begins with letter that you are emphasizing.

NOTES:

Letter Z Investigations:

- **Learn about zebras.**
- **Learn about the zoo.**
- **Learn about zinnias.**
- **Learn about zippers.**
- **Learn about zeros.**

Art:

⇒ Draw or paint zigzag lines.

⇒ Make a model of a zoo using shoeboxes to make different areas for animals.

⇒ Draw zebras.

⇒ Paint zeros.

Tactile:

* Fingerpaint "Z's" with different colors.

* Let children work with zippers, zipping them up and then down.

Baking:

◊ Roll cookie dough to form a long cord. Form the dough to make a zero.

Counting:

♥ Discuss what zero means.

♥ Draw zebras with different amounts of stripes (from 2 to 10). Let the children count the stripes and say the number. Write the number on the back of the picture for the children to see.

♥ Count the zippers in the room that day on clothing. Count the backpacks that have zippers.

Games:

Collect zippers for each child to use. Sing "Zipidy-Do-Da" and instruct children to zip or unzip only when they hear the word zip.

Fieldtrips and Special Days:
> Visit the zoo.

Books:

Zag, a Search through the Alphabet by Robert Tallon
Zoo Babies by Donna Grosvenor
Zoo, Where are You? by Ann McGovern
Zachary Goes to the Zoo by Jill Krementz
Put Me in the Zoo by Dr. Seuss

Songs:

Tune to: **"The Farmer in the Dell"**
Song: **"Zig-Zag"**

The zebra is in the zoo. The zebra is in the zoo.
Zig-zag and zoom, zoom, zoom; the zebra's in the zoo.

Tune to: **"He's Got the Whole World in His Hands"**
Song: **"How Many Zeros in a Zillion?"**

How many zeros in a zillion?
Tell me, how many zeros in a zillion?
How many zeros in a zillion?
Zig-Zag, zoom, zoom, zoom!

Fingerplay:

Five zebras in a zoo--
(Wiggle five fingers.)

The first one said, "I need new shoes."
(Touch thumb.)

The second said, "I do, too!"
(Touch index finger.)

The third one said, "My name is Sue."
(Touch middle finger.)

The fourth one said, "It's nice to meet you."
(Shake ring finger with other hand as if shaking hands.)

The Fifth one said, "How do you do?"
(Wiggle little finger.)

Poem:

I zip my zipper way up high.
It's hard to do, but I will try!
And later, when there's no more light,
I unzip my zipper and say goodnight!

Always acknowledge children whose first or last name begins with letter that you are emphasizing.

NOTES:

Fingerplay:

I'll Get You 'Squita

By Janie Allen-Bradley

Buzz-z-z, buz-z-z, buz-z-z!
What do I hear?
It's a mosquito.
Get away from my ear!

I'll get you, 'Squita.
I'll clap you in my hand.
Clap! Clap! Clap!

I'll get you, 'Squita.
I'll swat you as you sit.
Swat! Swat! Swat!
Why won't you let me hit?

I'll get you, 'Squita.
I'll squirt you with spray.
Squirt! Squirt! Squirt!
Why won't you go away?

I'll get you, 'Squita.
I'll step on you.
Step! Step! Step!
Why won't you shoo?

I'll get you, 'Squita.
I'll chase you home.
Chase! Chase! Chase!
Why won't you be gone?

I'll get you, 'Squita.
I'll.................
Oh! OUCH!
Why did YOU get me?

Involvement:

➢ Make motions to go with the poem.

➢ Write each verse on chart paper. Point to the words while reading. Encourage children to "read" along.

➢ Underline repetitive words with the same color.

➢ Make flash cards to match with the words.

➢ Make sentence strips to match whole lines, especially the ones beginning with "Why."

➢ Read <u>Why Mosquitoes Buzz in People's Ears</u> by Verna Aardema

Paint, Playdough, Recipes, and Other Fun Stuff:

☺ **Finger Paint**
What you need:
1/2 cup liquid starch
1/2 cup soap powder
5/8 cup water
Tempera paint

Beat together until the consistency of whipped potatoes. Have fun!

☺ **Face Paint**
1/8 C. baby lotion
1/4 tsp. powdered Tempera paint
1 squirt liquid dishwashing soap

Easily removed by soap and water.

☺ **Silly Putty**
Mix well
1 cup white glue
1 ½ cups liquid starch

☺ **Colored Paste**
2 parts salt
1 part flour
powdered paint & Water

Mix salt and flour. Add powdered paint. Slowly stir in enough water to make a smooth, heavy paste. This mix can be used like regular paste. Store in airtight container.

☺ **Goop**
Mix together food coloring, 1 cup cornstarch and 1 cup of water. Fun, Fun, Fun!

☺ **To Dye Egg shells, rice, & noodles**
Add a small amount of rubbing alcohol and food color together. Put materials in ziplock bag and mix with color. Put on paper towel and dry. Clean eggs with soap and water before using.

☺ **Puff Paint**
1 part self-rising flour
1 part salt
1 part water with color

Mix with beater & put into mustard/ketchup squeeze containers. Let children squeeze out to make picture.

☺ **Cornstarch Clay**
1 cup cornstarch
1/3 cup vegetable oil
2/3 cup flour
Pour cornstarch into a bowl and add oil and stir. Slowly add flour until thick and doughy. Knead well and store in airtight container.

☺ **Funny Feeling Playdough**
2 cups baking soda
1 ½ cups water
1 cup cornstarch

Mix with a fork until
smooth. Boil over med.
Heat until thick. Spoon onto
plate or wax paper.

☺ **Playdough**
2 ½ cups flour
½ cup salt
1 T alum
1 ¾ cup boiling water
2 T vegetable oil
Food coloring

Mix flour and salt in a bowl.
Mix alum, water, oil, and
food coloring in a separate
bowl and add to flour
mixture. Knead well. Add
more flour if sticky. Keep in
sealed container.

☺ **Salt Dough**
1 cup salt
4 cups flour
1 ½ cups water
4 T oil

Mix flour and salt. Add
water and oil slowly to the
dry ingredients. Mix well.
Knead dough until soft and
pliable. Bake 50 minutes at

300 degrees until hard. Paint
with acrylic or varnish to
seal.

☺ **Snow**
1 part Ivory Snow Detergent
½ part water

Beat with mixer until fluffy
and white. Great for
creating a crazy cake or
snow for an igloo.

☺ **Cookie Paint**
1 well beaten egg yolk
1/4 t. water

Mix and add food color
Paint on cookies or
biscuits with small
brushes. Do not let
cookies brown.

☺ **Learning about Color**
Pour milk to cover bottom of
glass bowl. Let each child
drop one drop of food color
into milk. Add one drop of
dishwashing detergent to
side of dish. Be ready to
watch!

☺ **Pumpkin Pie**
My Mother's secret recipe
It has been tried and proven to be delicious by my kindergarten.
1 can Libby's pie filling
2 eggs slightly beaten
1 cup sugar (The Secret)
1 can evaporated milk
2 t. pumpkin pie spice
Mix everything and pour into pie shell and cook at 350 degrees for about 1 hr.

☺ **Pizzas**
1 pkg. of hamburger buns
a small can of pizza sauce
Mozzarella cheese
Spread sauce on buns
Optional: olives, pepperoni
Sprinkle with cheese
Put under broiler for a few minutes.

☺ **Cake Cookies**
1 pkg. Yellow Cake Mix
1 stick of butter/oleo
1 egg
1 tsp of vanilla

Lightly grease cookie sheets. Mix all ingredients until dough forms. Roll out dough and cut with cookie cutters to desired shape or scoop dough with a spoon, press down and place on sheet. Bake at 350 in preheated oven. Bake 10 minutes. Take out and cool. Frosting is optional.

☺ **Honeybutter**
Beat softened oleo with one tablespoon of honey.

☺ **Edible Playdough**
1 cup peanut butter
1 cup non-fat dry milk
1 tablespoon honey

Mix altogether and mold into bears.

☺ **Quick Pie for Over-Extended Teachers!**
Soften 8 chocolate bars with almonds in microwave. DO NOT OVER HEAT!
Fold into bowl of large cool whip and pour into precooked pie shell. Put in freezer.

☺ **Dreamy Desert**
Soften 8 chocolate candy bars. Fold candy bars with large bowl of Cool Whip. Serve in small paper cups with spoon.

MOVING BOOKS

Plate Book

1. Cut triangular section out of paper plate.

2. Take poster board and trace plate on it.

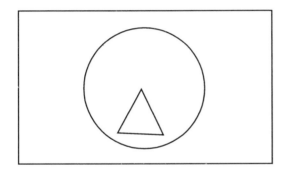

3. Brad plate to center and design book to teach your objective.

colors
numbers
shapes
opposites
matching

Decorate the board.

4. Make cards that children can draw from on the side and, the children can turn the wheel to find the corresponding color, number, shape, etc.

Talking Book

1. Fold manilla paper in half.

2. Go down about 2 inches.

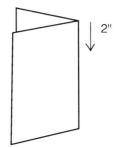

3. Cut straight about 1 1/2 inches.

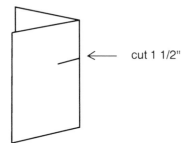

4. Fold and make two triangles. Move triangles back and forth 3 or 4 times.

 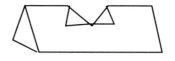

5. Pull the triangles to the inside and open.

Use your imagination.

Shape Book

Make books in different forms.

1. Cut out shape you want for front and back of book.

2. Cut out same shape for inside on either writing paper or plain paper for children to put picture on. They can cut out pictures and/ or illustrate the book themselves.

3. Staple on one side or put rings through book to hold together.

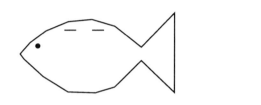 

Large Present

1. Fold piece of construction paper in half and cut apart on the crease.

 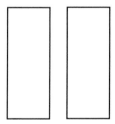

2. On one piece of paper, draw a box for a present and cut an opening in the box as shown.

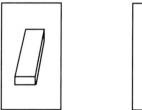 

3. On the other piece of paper, draw a surprise to be in the present. Glue the two pieces of paper together so that the surprise shows when you open the slit on the present. Give clues as to what is inside the present and have children guess.

Large or Tall Book

1. Fold construction paper and typing paper together. Staple on side.

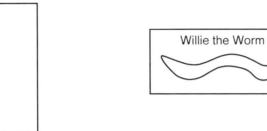

    Children can draw pictures or cut out pictures in book. Some may write words.

Surprise Book

1. Cut a shape out of construction paper.
   For example, if you cut out a house, make the door and windows be flaps.

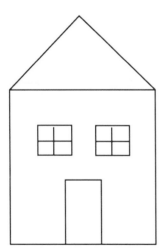

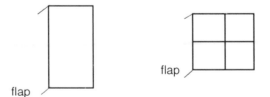

Make flaps on anything that can be moved and glued to picture.

    Ideas: look behind trees
             under rug
             behind a rock in ocean
             behind a picture
             in a closet

Flip Books

1. Book cover is made from an 8 1/2 x 11" tag board.

2. Staple several pieces of white construction paper together in two sets.

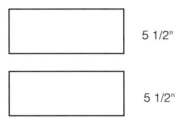

5 1/2"

5 1/2"

3. Make pictures for top and bottom that can go together or maybe will be silly looking.

example: A. Hats on top with faces on bottom

B. Pictures of things on top with corresponding numbers on bottom

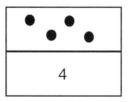

C. Rhyming pictures

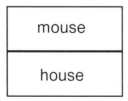

4. Staple construction paper together for cover and design.

Pop-up Book

1. Fold paper.

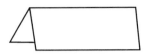

2. Find the center of the fold and on either side, cut down 2 inches. (This should look like a loose tooth.)

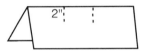

3. Fold flap back and forth a couple of times. (Wiggle the loose tooth).

4. Go in from the inside and pull that loose tooth to the inside all the way. Press on fold to crease.

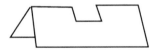

5. Open inside sheet and you should have a crisp step.

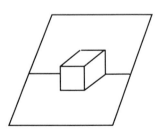

6. Glue anything to base of step.
   *Apply little glue to base of step and apply picture. (If too much glue is put on step, it could seep out and you'll never be able to open your book).

7. Add additional pages and construction paper for cover.

Holiday Fingerplays and Songs:
Halloween Song (Tune to "I Love to Go Awandering")

I love to go trick or treating on Halloween night.
And as I go, I always know the safety rules for me!

Chorus:
Hal-lo-ween, Hal-lo-ween, Hal-lo-ween
Hal-lo-weeeeeeeeeeeeen, Hal-lo-ween, Hal-lo-ween
Halloween is lots of fun!

(Hal-lo-weeeeeeeeeeeeen should be sung like a witch would.)
I know, I must go with an adult, and wear light colored clothes.
My parents always check my bag before I begin to eat.
(Chorus)

Thanksgiving Song (Tune to "Twinkle, Twinkle Little Star")

Turkey, turkey where are you?
I'm a pilgrim looking for you.
Thanksgiving Day is coming soon.
A Thanksgiving feast we'll have at noon.
(Repeat first two lines)

Christmas Song: (Tune to "Jimmy Crack Corn")

Santa's coming Christmas Day.
Santa's coming Christmas Day.
Santa's coming Christmas Day.
Tell me what he'll say! (Children respond loudly **"HO, HO, HO"**)
(Christmas wrapping paper: Let children place their handprints on butcher paper using red and green finger-paint.)

Columbus Day (Tune to "Oh, Do You Know the Muffin Man?")

Columbus sailed the ocean blue, the ocean blue, the ocean blue.
Columbus sailed the ocean blue in 1492.

Valentine Song (Tune to "Someone's in the Kitchen with Dinah")

Will you be my Valentine? Will you be my Valentine?
Will you be my Valentine, if you are wearing red!

*Substitute last line. Children will stand if they have the
item in the song on.*
➤ *If you are wearing sandals*
➤ *If you are wearing socks*
➤ *If you have tennis shoes on*
➤ *If you have brown eyes*
➤ *If your hair is blonde*

Valentine Bingo

Buy a bag of heart candy with Valentine sayings on each piece.
Choose 20-25 ones with different sayings, and put in a bag. Put in
another bag all the extras that match the first 20-25 ones that you have
choosen. Give each child 5 pieces on a paper plate or napkin. Draw
from your original selection. Children turn their piece over or put in
center of the plate when they have a match with what the teacher calls
out. When a child Bingo's, the child will call out Valentine! Children
eat candy after game.

Mother's Day

by Mary Jo Ayres

On Mother's Day, I give my adoration
For someone who has made her daily vocation.
Of loving, sharing, and caring for me,
And never thought about charging a fee!

So not just today, Dear Mother, I honor you;
But each and every day through!

Happy Mother's Day

Mother's Day Poem (Children may apply hand print)

Long Vowel Songs:

Tune to: **"London Bridge"**
Song: **"Amy Ate an Apricot"**

Amy ate an apricot, apricot, apricot.
Amy ate an apricot in April of this year.
Amy knows her ABC's, ABC's, ABC's.
Amy knows her ABC's and she knows her age.

(Substitute Abe for second verse.)

Sing "It's Not Easy" from the "More Natural Learning Songs from A-Z" cassette.

Tune to: **"The Farmer in the Dell"**
Song: **"I Have an Idea!"**

I have an idea. I have an idea.
On an island we will play and ice cream for us all.

Sing "Ode to "O" from the "More Natural Learning Songs from A-Z" cassette.

Tune to: **"Frog Went A Courtin'"**
Song: **"There's No Unicorn in the USA."**

There's no unicorn in the USA.
There's no unicorn in the USA.
If you look all over the universe,
there's not one unicorn you would see.
There's no unicorn in the USA.

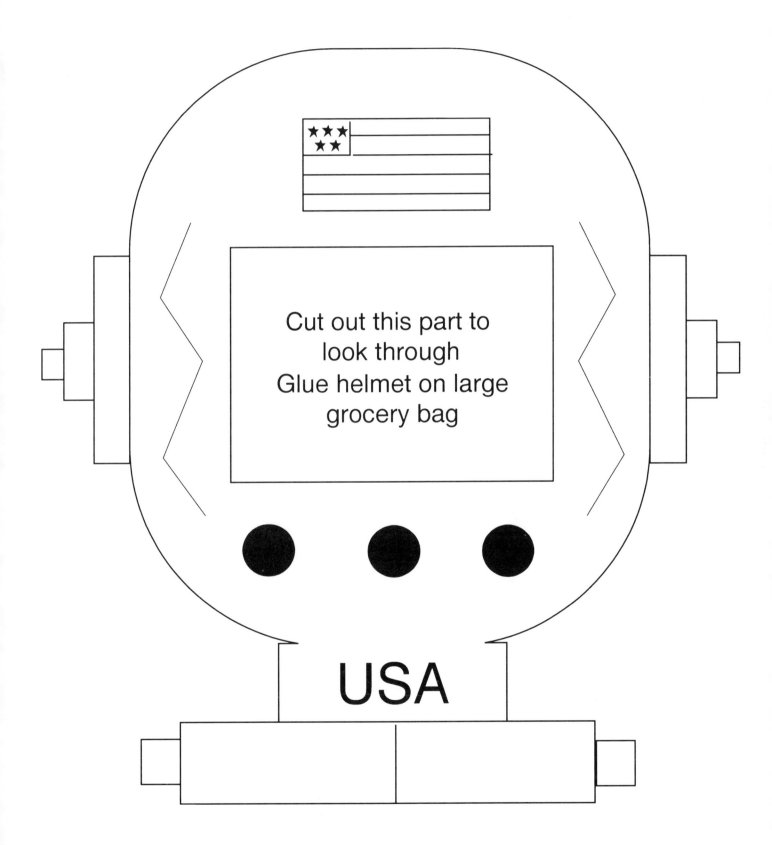

Cut out this part to
look through
Glue helmet on large
grocery bag

USA

Let children cut out
dog and write "D"
on tag.

DOG

Elephant Puppet

Cut hole in cardboard 7" by 7".

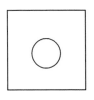

Pull sock through and cut 3 (3") cuts
spread sock and hot glue.

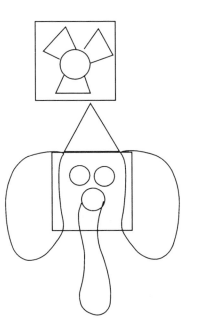

Long part of sock hangs out front.

Add ears, eyes, and circus hat.

On back of ear put poem:

>I'm an elephant big and gray.
>See my trunk sway this way!
>In circus I may be
>With a hat for you to see!

elephant ear
cut 2

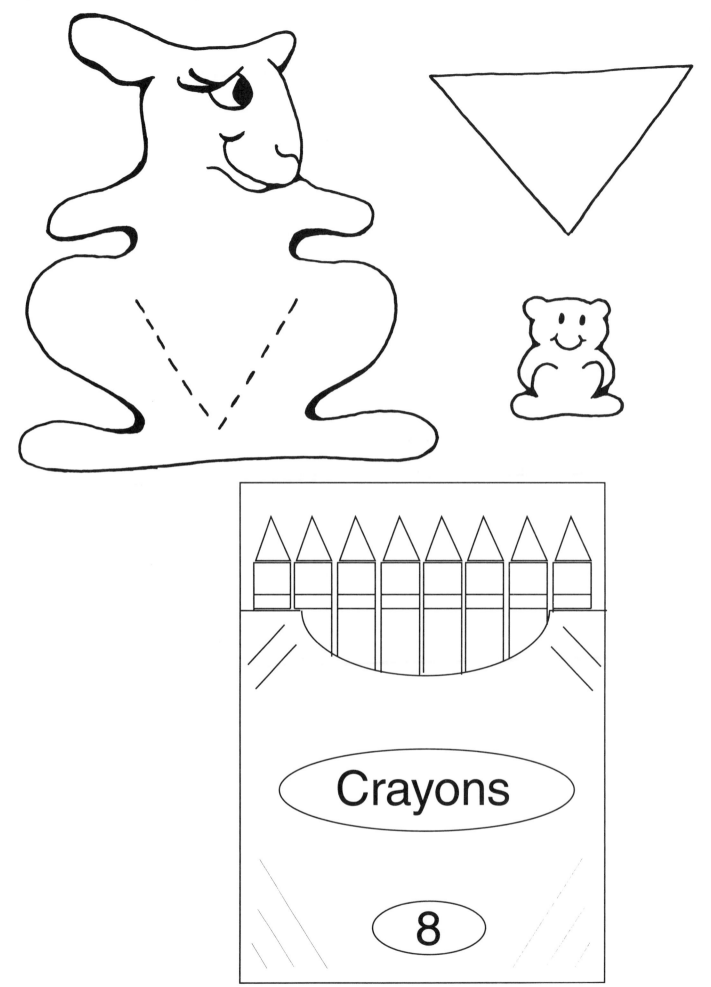

Crayons

8

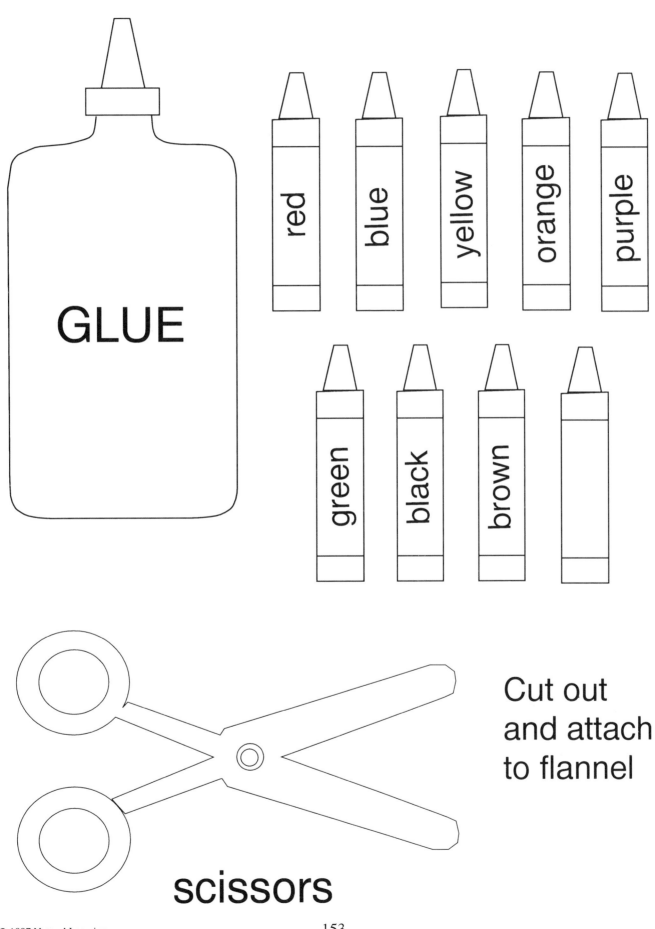

GLUE

red

blue

yellow

orange

purple

green

black

brown

Cut out
and attach
to flannel

scissors

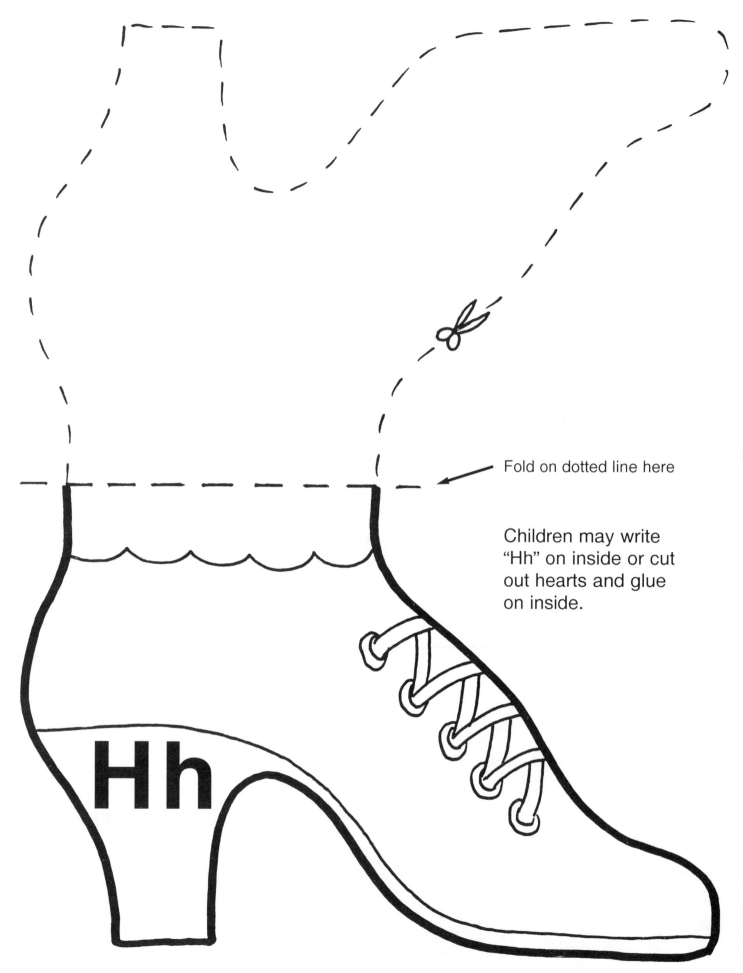

Fold on dotted line here

Children may write "Hh" on inside or cut out hearts and glue on inside.

Hh

Letter V

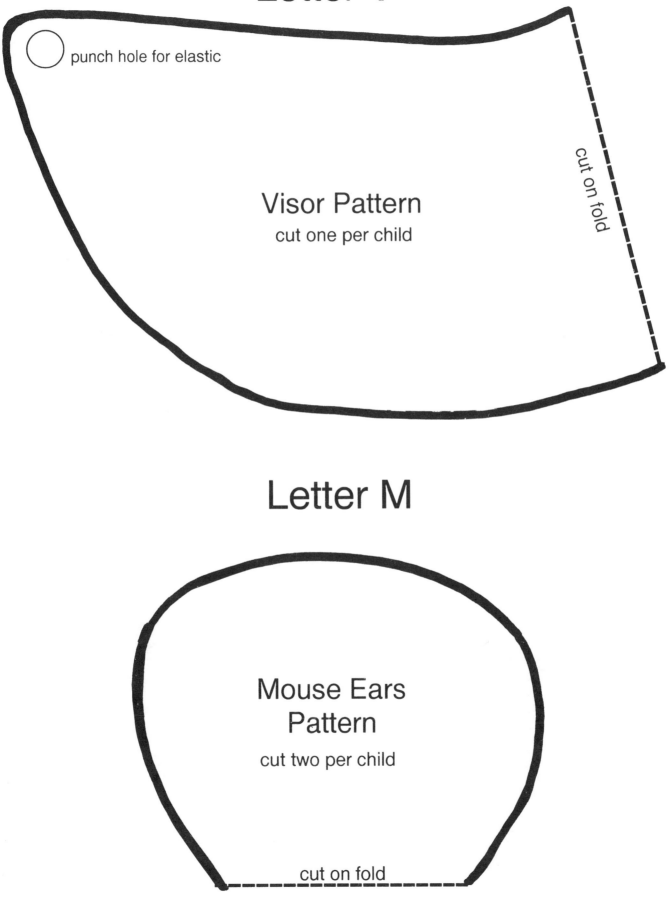

punch hole for elastic

Visor Pattern

cut one per child

cut on fold

Letter M

**Mouse Ears
Pattern**

cut two per child

cut on fold

10 Toads

wallet

$1
dollar

1 one
George
Washington

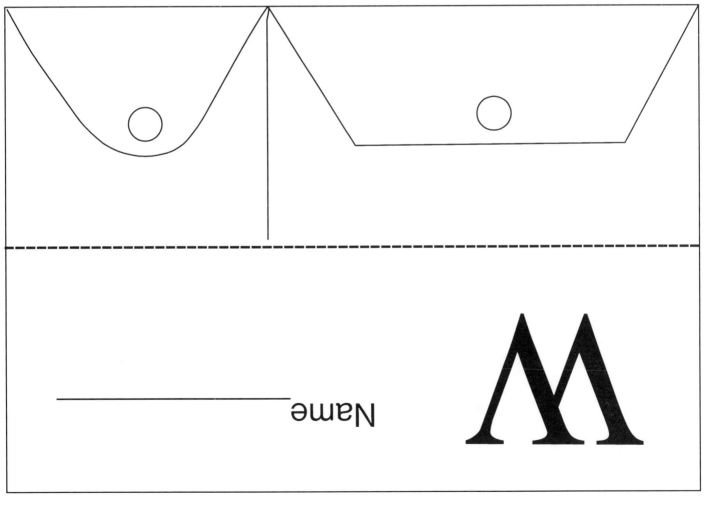

Name _____

fold in center   glue only on sides

157

Name _____

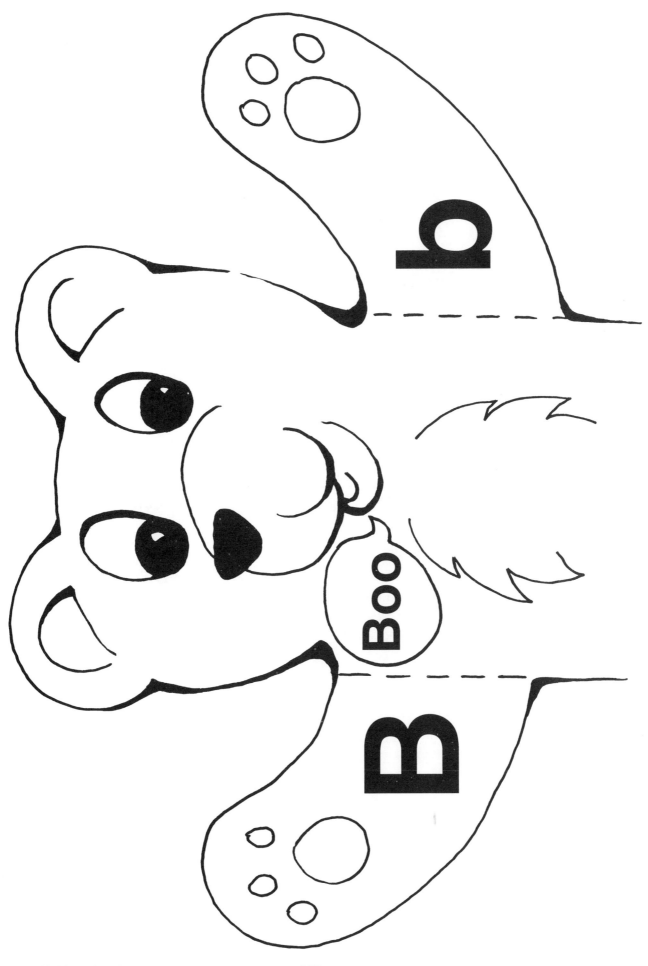

Order Form

Fax order: 601-686-2365

Postal orders: Natural Learning
                      103 Sycamore St.
                      Leland, MS 38756

Book:

☐ Natural Learning From A-Z $19.95

Cassette:

☐ Happy Teaching & Natural Learning Songs from A-Z $10.00

☐ More Natural Learning Songs from A-Z $10.00

Puppet:

☐ Ms Magnolia puppet $25.00

Subtotal _____

Sales tax:

Please add 7% for books shipped to Mississippi addresses.   _____

Shipping:

$4.00 for first book and $2.00 for each additional book.   S&H   _____

$3.00 for first cassette and $1.50 for each additional cassette.

$4.00 for book and cassette order.

$4.00 for Ms Magnolia.   Total

(For combined orders please call 601-686-9691)

Payment:

E-mail address:_____

☐ Check   (optional)

Credit Card:

Name:_____

☐ VISA

Address:_____

☐ MasterCard

City:_____ State_____ Zip_____

Card Number:_____

Name on Card:_____

Exp. Date:_____/_____

Signature:_____